George Herbert

The Works of
George Herbert

with an Introduction by Dr. Tim Cook,
and Bibliography

Wordsworth Poetry Library

This edition published 1994 by Wordsworth Editions Ltd,
Cumberland House, Crib Street, Ware, Hertfordshire SG12 9ET.

ISBN 1-85326-421-0

Typeset in the UK by Antony Gray.
Printed and bound in Denmark by Nørhaven.

The paper in this book is produced from pure wood
pulp, without the use of chlorine or any other substance
harmful to the environment. The energy used in its
production consists almost entirely of hydroelectricity
and heat generated from waste materials, thereby
conserving fossil fuels and contributing little to the
greenhouse effect.

INTRODUCTION

George Herbert, who was born in 1593, was a distant cousin of the well-known aristocratic patron of Elizabethan poets, William Herbert Earl of Pembroke, the nephew of Sir Philip Sidney. His mother, Magdalen Herbert, a friend of John Donne's, was admired for her Christian virtues, and the young Herbert seems from the first to have been influenced by her devoutness. Although he would have known and valued the political achievements of Sidney and probably those of Donne in his witty and highly intellectual love poetry, Herbert made it clear in two very early sonnets ('My God, where is that ancient heat towards Thee?' and 'Sure, Lord there is enough in Thee to dry') sent to his mother that he felt the proper subject of poetry was not relations between man and woman but man's relationship with God.

At first, however, his career seemed likely to follow the normal pattern of a talented young man with aristocratic connections. He distinguished himself at Cambridge and attracted the favourable attention of James I. He also served for a while as a Member of Parliament. However, with the accession of Charles I in 1625, and with his health, which had never been good, becoming more uncertain, he seems to have decided that his real future lay in the religious life. He was eventually given the living of Bemerton, near Salisbury, in 1630, and devoted himself wholeheartedly to his work as a country parson for three years until his health gave way and he died in 1633. The events of his life later became the subject of a somewhat embellished biography of him by his acquaintance Izaak Walton, with the apparent intention of providing Anglicanism with a ready-made saint of its own.

In his later years, besides writing a brief handbook giving a very personal view of the role and responsibilities of a parish priest (*A Priest to the Temple, or The Country Parson*), Herbert also produced his masterpiece, *The Temple*, a book of poems reflecting on various aspects of Christian life and ritual and exploring the vicissitudes of his own relationship with God. Some of the poems take as their starting point the fabric and contents of a church, or the key dates in the Christian year, meditating on their symbolic meaning. Many, on the other hand, can be seen as love poems, in their way every bit as passionate and varied as the *Sonnets* of Shakespeare or the lyrics of Herbert's family friend John Donne.

In the two 'Jordan' poems, for instance, he argues, as he did in his early sonnets, that the proper use of language is to celebrate and praise God, not to waste one's skill in it, as his predecessors did, on praising impermanent feminine beauty. 'Jordan I' mocks the convention of Petrarchan love poetry, while 'Jordan II' rewrites the opening sonnet of Sidney's *Astrophil and Stella*, in which the poet searches for inspiration. Whereas Sidney is told by his Muse to look into his heart where he keeps the image of his beloved, Herbert's search for 'rich' words is resolved by the friendly voice of the Holy Spirit reminding him that all the sweetness he needs is to be found in God's love.

In 'Deniall', Herbert takes the situation of the cruel mistress, deaf to her lover's pleas, a common theme (found, for instance, in Sir Thomas Wyatt's 'My Lute Awake'), and adapts it to convey the despair of the sinner trying to make contact with God. He combines images drawn from archery and music as the bow shooting his prayers at an apparently unhearing target breaks and produces discord, reflected in stanzas that fail to rhyme properly. Finally, harmony and full rhyme are restored at the end as the supplicant recognises his own 'heartlesse breast' and appeals for help. The disharmony expressed through disrupted rhyme sounds in 'Deniall' is shown visually in the, at first sight, chaotic medley of short and long lines in 'The Collar', a poem not of despair but of outright rebellion ('choler' – an aural pun) against the religious life, with the speaker tugging violently at the leash that holds him until suddenly subdued, as in 'Jordan II', by the quiet voice of heavenly love. In 'Discipline' we see him, in contrast, addressing God in short, pleading, almost hesitant lines, reminding him that love and gentle treatment can have as much power to move the sinner as severity.

On the other hand there are poems in which there is a sense of love regained or returned. One of the most powerful of these is 'The Flower' in which the poet compares the recovery of a sense of being in touch with God to the effect of Spring on the natural world, with his 'shrivel'd heart' recovering 'greennesse' like withered bulbs or roots underground. Yet he is aware that this sense of being loved is impermanent in this life, since his sins may bring about more frosts in the relationship, and he longs for the ultimate, eternal garden of Paradise. Once again the wintry image is similar to that used in the Petrarchan tradition about estrangements in human relationships.

Herbert grew up in a world in which books of visual emblems with moral significance for those capable of interpreting them were popular, and a number of his poems besides 'The Collar' express their meaning through their form as well as their content. 'The Pearl', for example, can be compared in its argument with love poems by Donne, Sidney and others in which the lover is reproached by a critic for neglecting his worldly duties for the sake of his love. Herbert instead lists all that the world has to offer by way of fame through honour and learning, as well as through pleasure, in three large regular stanzas each dominating a tiny refrain of four words expressing the love for God, the pearl of great price, which has made him abandon worldly temptations. The matching concluding stanza shows a poet fully aware what he is rejoicing and yet asserting that those seemingly insignificant words of love more than match in worth the bulky stanzas to which they are attached. The love of God becomes the silken thread by which Theseus in the classical legend was enabled to escape the Minotaur, easily identifiable by Herbert's readers with the Devil.

Another poem, 'Easter Wings', expresses through its form the wings of faith through which the soul may reach Heaven, and through its diminishing and lengthening lines the fall and redemption of humanity in general and the individual in particular. The poem 'Our Life Is Hid with Christ in God' has a text from St Paul about the spiritual life concealed diagonally in a stanza meditating on the relationship between that life and our daily existence. The two brief lines of another poem explore the reason why Mary is an anagram of 'army', since for Herbert such a fact must have a significance given it by God for Christians to explore. Another use of the meanings hidden in the letters that make up words is found in the poem 'Paradise' where the rhyme word in a poem of garden images is 'pruned' in each stanza by one letter a line.

Herbert is perpetually meditating on the significance of the objects from his everyday life. He explains to his reader how the Christian virtues can be learnt, for example, from the chequered pattern on 'The Church Floor' while in 'Life' he makes a posy of flowers he has gathered emblematic of the transience of human life, seeing it as a positive good in contrast with those secular poets who use the ephemeral nature of the beauty of flowers to persuade their mistresses to make good use of time for pleasure. The idea that even the simplest and humblest actions, such as sweeping a room, can be given religious significance if approached in the right frame of mind is the subject of 'The Elixir', a poem that makes use of the alchemical imagery associated with Donne.

Perhaps one of the most moving of all Herbert's poems, and one that brings out most clearly the tensions between the poet and the Christian in his work, is 'The Forerunners'. Here his concern, as in 'The Flower', is with his advancing age (though he was under forty). We find him meditating on the white hairs which are 'harbingers' of death, worrying about the effect of age on his mental powers, and particularly on his ability to continue writing poems worthy of his divine subject. He asks movingly if he will really have to bid farewell to his 'Lovely enchanting language', leaving it to the love-poets to misuse on the 'dung' of mortal human beauty. Although he seems firmly resigned to the loss of his gifts and inspiration, assuring us that all that really matters is that his faith remains steadfast, it is a poem that shows poignantly how deeply he valued his literary gifts and how much of a consolation he found them for the disappointments of life.

Yet in the end it was his relationship with God, and particularly with Christ as Redeemer, that really mattered to him. At the end of The Temple he placed a poem, simply called 'Love', that uses the symbolism of the Communion table to express his confidence that, despite his unworthiness, there will be a place for him amongst the ranks of the elect. It is one of his least complex, most domestic poems and one of his most effective.

For Christians it will be easy, once they have become accustomed to his language and habits of thought, to appreciate Herbert's achievement. However, in an age much less preoccupied with religious matters than Herbert's seventeenth century, at least in Europe, many readers will find the subject-matter of his poetry alien and remote.

Such readers, perhaps the majority in England today, may still see in his poems the varying moods of someone exploring a difficult but often deeply rewarding relationship, using unusual images (or, as Renaissance poets would have called them, 'conceits') in many ingenious ways and showing remarkable skill in devising appropriate stanza forms. His work can be read and reread, and new subtleties in language and imagery discovered at each reading. Although dismissed as 'quaint' by some critics in the centuries after his death, The Temple has deeply influenced later religious poets, such as Gerard Manley Hopkins, and George Herbert is one of the older English poets most admired by practising modern poets, whether they share his faith or not.

Dr Tim Cook
Kingston University

FURTHER READING

I. Walton: The Life of Mr George Herbert
R. Tuve: A Reading of George Herbert
J. Summers: George Herbert, His Religion and Art
L. Martz: The Poetry of Meditation
S. Fish: The Living Temple
R. Todd: The Opacity of Signs

CONTENTS

THE TEMPLE

THE CHURCH MILITANT

ADDITIONAL SACRED POEMS

PSALMS

SECULAR POEMS

THE TEMPLE

I THE DEDICATION

Lord, my first-fruits present themselves to Thee;
Yet not mine neither; for from Thee they came,
And must return. Accept of them and me,
And make us strive who shall sing best Thy Name.
   Turn their eyes hither who shall make a gain;
   Theirs who shall hurt themselves or me refrain.

II THE CHURCH PORCH

Perirrhanterium

I
Thou whose sweet youth and early hopes inhance
Thy rate and price, and mark thee for a treasure,
Hearken unto a Verser, who may chance
Ryme thee to good, and make a bait of pleasure:
   A verse may finde him who a sermon flies,
   And turn delight into a sacrifice.

II
Beware of lust; it doth pollute and foul
Whom God in Baptisme washt with His own Bloud;
It blots thy lesson written in thy soul;
The holy lines cannot be understood:
   How dare those eyes upon a Bible look,
   Much lesse towards God, whose lust is all their book!

III
Abstain wholly, or wed. Thy bounteous Lord
Allows thee choise of paths; take no by-wayes,
But gladly welcome what He doth afford,
Not grudging that thy lust hath bounds and staies.
   Continence hath his joy; weigh both, and so,
   If rottennesse have more, let Heaven go.

IV

If God had laid all common, certainly
Man would have been th' incloser; but since now
God hath impal'd us, on the contrarye
Man breaks the fence, and every ground will plough.
   O, what were man, might he himself misplace!
   Sure, to be crosse, he would shift feet and face.

V

Drink not the third glasse, – which thou canst not tame
When once it is within thee, but before
Mayst rule it as thou list, – and poure the shame,
Which it would poure on thee, upon the floore.
   It is most just to throw that on the ground
   Which would throw me there if I keep the round.

VI

He that is drunken, may his mother kill
Bigge with his sister: he hath lost the reins,
Is outlawd by himselfe; all kinds of ill
Did with his liquor slide into his veins.
   The drunkard forfets Man, and doth devest
   All worldly right, save what he hath by beast.

VII

Shall I, to please another's wine-sprung minde,
Lose all mine own? God hath giv'n me a measure
Short of his canne and bodie; must I finde
A pain in that wherein he findes a pleasure?
   Stay at the third glasse; if thou lose thy hold,
   Then thou art modest, and the wine grows bold.

VIII

If reason move not gallants, quit the room –
All in a shipwrack shift their severall way;
Let not a common ruine thee intombe:
Be not a beast in courtesie, but stay, –
   Stay at the third cup, or forgo the place:
   Wine above all things doth God's stamp deface.

IX

Yet, if thou sinne in wine or wantonnesse,
Boast not thereof, nor make thy shame thy glorie.
Frailtie gets pardon by submissivenesse;
But he that boasts shuts that out of his storie;
    He makes flat warre with God, and doth defie
    With his poore clod of earth the spacious skie.

X

Take not His Name, Who made thy mouth, in vain;
It gets thee nothing, and hath no excuse.
Lust and wine plead a pleasure, avarice gain;
But the cheap swearer through his open sluce
    Lets his soul runne for nought, as little fearing:
    Were I an Epicure, could bate swearing.

XI

When thou dost tell another's jest, therein
Omit the oathes, which true wit cannot need;
Pick out of tales the mirth, but not the sinne;
He pares his apple that will cleanly feed.
    Play not away the vertue of that Name
    Which is the best stake when griefs make thee tame.

XII

The cheapest sinnes most dearly punisht are,
Because to shun them also is so cheap;
For we have wit to mark them, and to spare.
O, crumble not away thy soul's fair heap!
    If thou wilt die, the gates of hell are broad;
    Pride and full sinnes have made the way a road.

XIII

Lie not; but let thy heart be true to God,
Thy mouth to it, thy actions to them both:
Cowards tell lies, and those that fear the rod;
The stormie-working soul spits lies and froth.
    Dare to be true: nothing can need a ly;
    A fault, which needs it most, grows two thereby.

XIV

Flie idlenesse; which yet thou canst not flie
By dressing, mistressing, and complement.
If those take up thy day, the sunne will crie
Against thee; for his light was onely lent.
God gave thy soul brave wings; put not those feathers
Into a bed, to sleep out all ill weathers.

XV

Art thou a magistrate? then be severe:
If studious, copie fair what Time hath blurr'd,
Redeem truth from his jawes: if souldier,
Chase brave employments with a naked sword
Throughout the world. Fool not; for all may have,
If they dare try, a glorious life, or grave.

XVI

O England, full of sinne, but most of sloth!
Spit out thy flegme, and fill thy breast with glorie.
Thy gentry bleats, as if thy native cloth
Transfus'd a sheepishnesse into thy storie;
Not that they all are so, but that the most
Are gone to grasse, and in the pasture lost.

XVII

This losse springs chiefly from our education:
Some till their ground, but let weeds choke their sonne;
Some mark a partridge, never their childe's fashion;
Some ship them over, and the thing is done.
Studie this art, make it thy great designe;
And if God's image move thee not, let thine.

XVIII

Some great estates provide, but do not breed
A mast'ring minde; so both are lost thereby.
Or els they breed them tender, make them need
All that they leave; this is flat povertie:
For he that needs five thousand pound to live
Is full as poore as he that needs but five.

XIX

The way to make thy sonne rich is to fill
His minde with rest, before his trunk with riches:
For wealth without contentment climbes a hill,
To feel those tempests which fly over ditches;
    But if thy sonne can make ten pound his measure,
    Then all thou addest may be call'd his treasure.

XX

When thou dost purpose ought within thy power,
Be sure to doe it, though it be but small;
Constancie knits the bones, and makes us stowre
When wanton pleasures becken, us to thrall.
    Who breaks his own bond forfeiteth himself;
    What nature made a ship, he makes a shelf.

XXI

Doe all things like a man, not sneakingly;
Think the king sees thee still; for his King does.
Simpring is but a lay-hypocrisie;
Give it a corner, and the clue undoes.
    Who fears to do ill sets himself to task;
    Who fears to do well sure should wear a mask.

XXII

Look to thy mouth; diseases enter there.
Thou hast two sconses: if thy stomach call,
Carve, or discourse; do not a famine fear:
Who carves is kind to two; who talks, to all.
    Look on meat, think it dirt, then eat a bit,
    And say withall, – 'Earth to earth I commit.'

XXIII

Slight those who say, amidst their sickly healths,
'Thou liv'st by rule.' What doth not so but man?
Houses are built by rule, and Common-Wealths.
Entice the trusty sunne, if that you can,
    From his ecliptick line; becken the skie!
    Who lives by rule, then, keeps good companie.

XXIV

Who keeps no guard upon himself is slack,
And rots to nothing at the next great thaw.
Man is a shop of rules, a well-truss'd pack,
Whose every parcell under-writes a law.
 Loose not thyself, nor give thy humours way;
 God gave them to thee under lock and key.

XXV

By all means use sometimes to be alone;
Salute thyself; see what thy soul doth wear;
Dare to look in thy chest, for 'tis thine own,
And tumble up and down what thou find'st there:
 Who cannot rest till he good-fellows finde,
 He breaks up house, turns out of doores his minde.

XXVI

Be thrifty, but not covetous: therefore give
Thy need, thine honour, and thy friend his due.
Never was scraper brave man. Get to live;
Then live, and use it; els it is not true
 That thou hast gotten. Surely use alone
 Makes money not a contemptible stone.

XXVII

Never exceed thy income. Youth may make
Ev'n with the yeare; but Age, if it will hit,
Shoots a bow short, and lessens still his stake,
As the day lessens, and his life with it.
 Thy children, kindred, friends upon thee call,
 Before thy journey fairly part with all.

XXVIII

Yet in thy thriving still misdoubt some evil,
Lest gaining gain on thee, and make thee dimme
To all things els. Wealth is the conjurer's devil,
Whom when he thinks he hath, the devil hath him.
 Gold thou mayst safely touch; but if it stick
 Unto thy hands, it woundeth to the quick.

XXIX

What skills it, if a bag of stones or gold
About thy neck do drown thee? Raise thy head;
Take starres for money, – starres not to be told
By any art, yet to be purchasèd.
 None is so wastfull as the scraping dame;
 Shee loseth three for one, – her soul, rest, fame.

XXX

By no means runne in debt: take thine own measure;
Who cannot live on twentie pound a yeare,
Cannot on fourtie; he's a man of pleasure,
A kinde of thing that's for itself too deere.
 The curious unthrift makes his cloth too wide,
 And spares himself, but would his taylor chide.

XXXI

Spend not on hopes. They that by pleading-clothes
Do fortunes seek when worth and service fail,
Would have their tale beleevèd for their oathes,
And are like empty vessels under sail.
 Old courtiers know this: therefore set out so,
 As all the day thou mayst hold out to go.

XXXII

In clothes, cheap handsomenesse doth bear the bell;
Wisedome's a trimmer thing then shop e'er gave.
Say not then, 'This with that lace will do well':
But, 'This with my discretion will be brave.'
 Much curiousnesse is a perpetuall wooing
 Nothing with labour, folly long a-doing.

XXXIII

Play not for gain, but sport. Who playes for more
Then he can lose with pleasure, stakes his heart;
Perhaps his wive's too, and whom she hath bore:
Servants and churches also play their part.
 Onely a herauld, who that way doth passe,
 Findes his crakt name at length in the church-glasse.

XXXIV

If yet thou love game at so deere a rate,
Learn this, that hath old gamesters deerly cost:
Dost lose? rise up; dost winne? rise in that state:
Who strive to sit out losing hands are lost.
　　Game is a civil gunpowder, in peace
　　Blowing up houses with their whole increase.

XXXV

In conversation boldnesse now bears sway:
But know, that nothing can so foolish be
As empty boldnesse: therefore first assay
To stuffe thy minde with solid braverie;
　　Then march on gallant: get substantiall worth;
　　Boldnesse guilds finely, and will set it forth.

XXXVI

Be sweet to all. Is thy complexion sowre?
Then keep such companie; make them thy allay;
Get a sharp wife, a servant that will lowre:
A stumbler stumbles least in rugged way.
　　Command thy self in chief. He life's warre knows,
　　Whom all his passions follow as he goes.

XXXVII

Catch not at quarrels. He that dares not speak
Plainly and home is coward of the two.
Think not thy fame at ev'ry twitch will break;
By great deeds show that thou canst little do, –
　　And do them not; that shall thy wisdome be;
　　And change thy temperance into braverie.

XXXVIII

If that thy fame with ev'ry toy be pos'd,
'Tis a thinne web, which poysonous fancies make.
But the great souldier's honour was compos'd
Of thicker stuffe, which would endure a shake.
　　Wisdome picks friends; civilitie playes the rest:
　　A toy shunn'd cleanly passeth with the best.

XXXIX

Laugh not too much; the wittie man laughs least;
For wit is newes only to ignorance.
Lesse at thine own things laugh, lest in the jest
Thy person share, and the conceit advance:
   Make not thy sport abuses; for the fly
   That feeds on dung is colourèd thereby.

XL

Pick out of mirth, like stones out of thy ground,
Profanenesse, filthinesse, abusivenesse;
These are the scumme, with which course wits abound:
The fine may spare these well, yet not go lesse.
   All things are bigge with jest; nothing that's plain
   But may be wittie, if thou hast the vein.

XLI

Wit's an unruly engine, wildly striking
Sometimes a friend, sometimes the engineer;
Hast thou the knack? pamper it not with liking;
But if thou want it, buy it not too deere.
   Many affecting wit beyond their power
   Have got to be a deare fool for an houre.

XLII

A sad wise valour is the brave complexion
That leads the van and swallowes up the cities.
The giggler is a milkmaid, whom infection
Or a fir'd beacon frighteth from his ditties:
   Then he's the sport; the mirth then in him rests,
   And the sad man is cock of all his jests.

XLIII

Towards great persons use respective boldnesse;
That temper gives them theirs, and yet doth take
Nothing from thine; in service, care or coldnesse
Doth ratably thy fortunes marre or make.
   Feed no man in his sinnes; for adulation
   Doth make thee parcell-devil in damnation.

XLIV

Envie not greatnesse; for thou mak'st thereby
Thyself the worse, and so the distance greater.
Be not thine own worm; yet such jealousie
As hurts not others, but may make thee better,
    Is a good spurre. Correct thy passions' spite;
    Then may the beasts draw thee to happy light.

XLV

When basenesse is exalted, do not bate
The place its honour for the person's sake;
The shrine is that which thou dost venerate,
And not the beast that bears it on his back.
    I care not though the cloth of state should be
    Not of rich arras but mean tapestrie.

XLVI

Thy friend put in thy bosome; wear his eies
Still in thy heart, that he may see what's there.
If cause require thou art his sacrifice,
Thy drops of bloud must pay down all his fear;
    But love is lost, the way of friendship's gone,
    Though David had his Jonathan, Christ his John.

XLVII

Yet be not surety, if thou be a father:
Love is a personall debt, I cannot give
My children's right, nor ought he take it: rather
Both friends should die then hinder them to live.
    Fathers first enter bonds to Nature's ends,
    And are her sureties ere they are a friend's.

XLVIII

If thou be single, all thy goods and ground
Submit to love; but yet not more then all:
Give one estate, as one life. None is bound
To work for two, who brought himself to thrall.
    God made me one man; love makes me no more,
    Till labour come and make my weaknesse score.

XLIX

In thy discourse, if thou desire to please,
All such is courteous, usefull, new, or wittie:
Usefulnesse comes by labour, wit by ease;
Courtesie grows in Court, news in the citie:
  Get a good stock of these, then draw the card
  That suites him best, of whom thy speech is heard.

L

Entice all neatly to what they know best;
For so thou dost thyself and him a pleasure; –
But a proud ignorance will lose his rest,
Rather then shew his cards; – steal from his treasure
  What to ask further: doubts well-rais'd do lock
  The speaker to thee, and preserve thy stock.

LI

If thou be master-gunner, spend not all
That thou canst speak at once, but husband it,
And give men turns of speech; do not forestall
By lavishnesse thine own and others' wit,
  As if thou mad'st thy will: a civil guest
  Will no more talk all then eat all the feast.

LII

Be calm in arguing; for fiercenesse makes
Errour a fault, and truth discourtesie.
Why should I feel another man's mistakes
More then his sicknesses or povertie?
  In love I should; but anger is not love,
  Nor wisdome neither; therefore gently move.

LIII

Calmnesse is great advantage; he that lets
Another chafe, may warm him at his fire,
Mark all his wandrings, and enjoy his frets,
As cunning fencers suffer heat to tire.
  Truth dwels not in the clouds; the bow that's there
  Doth often aim at, never hit the sphere.

LIV

Mark what another sayes; for many are
Full of themselves, and answer their own notion.
Take all into thee; then with equall care
Ballance each dramme of reason, like a potion.
 If truth be with thy friend, be with them both,
 Share in the conquest, and confesse a troth.

LV

Be useful where thou livest, that they may
Both want and wish thy pleasing presence still.
Kindnesse, good parts, great places, are the way
To compasse this. Finde out men's wants and will,
 And meet them there. All worldly joyes go lesse
 To the one joy of doing kindnesses.

LVI

Pitch thy behaviour low, thy projects high;
So shalt thou humble and magnanimous be:
Sink not in spirit; who aimeth at the sky
Shoots higher much then he that means a tree.
 A grain of glorie mixt with humblenesse
 Cures both a fever and lethargicknesse.

LVII

Let thy mind still be bent, still plotting where
And when and how the businesse may be done.
Slacknesse breeds worms; but the sure traveller,
Though he alight sometimes, still goeth on.
 Active and stirring spirits live alone;
 Write on the others 'HERE LIES SUCH A ONE.'

LVIII

Slight not the smallest losse, whether it be
In love or honour; take account of all:
Shine like the sunne in every corner: see
Whether thy stock of credit swell or fall.
 Who say 'I care not,' those I give for lost,
 And to instruct them 'twill not quit the cost.

LIX

Scorn no man's love, though of a mean degree, –
Love is a present for a mightie king;
Much lesse make any one thine enemie:
As gunnes destroy, so may a little sling.
  The cunning workman never doth refuse
  The meanest tool that he may chance to use.

LX

All forrain wisdome doth amount to this,
To take all that is given, whether wealth,
Or love, or language; nothing comes amisse;
A good digestion turneth all to health:
  And then, as farre as fair behaviour may,
  Strike off all scores; none are so cleare as they.

LXI

Keep all thy native good, and naturalize
All forrain of that name; but scorn their ill;
Embrace their activenesse, not vanities:
Who follows all things, forfeiteth his will.
  If thou observest strangers in each fit,
  In time they'l runne thee out of all thy wit.

LXII

Affect in things about thee cleanlinesse,
That all may gladly board thee, as a flowre.
Slovens take up their stock of noisomenesse
Beforehand, and anticipate their last houre.
  Let thy minde's sweetnesse have his operation
  Upon thy body, clothes, and habitation.

LXIII

In almes regard thy meanes and others' merit;
Think heav'n a better bargain then to give
Onely thy single market-money for it;
Joyn hands with God to make a man to live.
  Give to all something; to a good poore man
  Till thou change names, and be where he began.

LXIV

Man is God's image; but a poore man is
Christ's stamp to boot; both images regard.
God reckons for him, count the favour His;
Write 'So much giv'n to God': thou shalt be heard.
   Let thy almes goe before and keep heav'n's gate
   Open for thee; or both may come too late.

LXV

Restore to God His due in tithe and time;
A tithe purloin'd cankers the whole estate.
Sundaies observe; think when the bells do chime,
'Tis angels' musick; therefore come not late.
   God then deals blessings: if a king did so,
   Who would not haste, nay give, to see the show?

LXVI

Twice on that day His due is understood;
For all the week thy food so oft He gave thee.
Thy cheere is mended; bate not of the food,
Because 'tis better, and perhaps may save thee.
   Thwart not th' Almighty God: O, be not crosse!
   Fast when thou wilt; but then 'tis gain, not losse.

LXVII

Though private prayer be a brave designe,
Yet publick hath more promises, more love;
And love's a weight to hearts, to eies a signe.
We all are but cold suitours; let us move
   Where it is warmest: leave thy six and seven;
   Pray with the most, for where most pray is heaven.

LXVIII

When once thy foot enters the Church, be bare;
God is more there then thou; for thou art there
Onely by His permission: then beware,
And make thyself all reverence and fear.
   Kneeling ne're spoil'd silk stocking; quit thy state;
   All equall are within the Churche's gate.

LXIX

Resort to sermons, but to prayers most:
Praying's the end of preaching. O, be drest;
Stay not for th' other pin! Why, thou hast lost
A joy for it worth worlds. Thus Hell doth jest
  Away thy blessings, and extreamly flout thee;
  Thy clothes being fast, but thy soul loose about thee.

LXX

In time of service seal up both thine eies,
And send them to thine heart, that, spying sinne,
They may weep out the stains by them did rise:
Those doores being shut, all by the eare comes in.
  Who marks in church-time others' symmetrie
  Makes all their beautie his deformitie.

LXXI

Let vain or busie thoughts have there no part;
Bring not thy plough, thy plots, thy pleasures thither.
Christ purged His temple; so must thou thy heart:
All worldly thoughts are but theeves met together
  To couzin thee. Look to thy actions well;
  For churches are either our Heav'n or Hell.

LXXII

Judge not the preacher, for He is thy judge;
If thou mislike him, thou conceiv'st Him not:
God calleth preaching folly: do not grudge
To pick out treasures from an earthen pot:
  The worst speak something good; if all want sense,
  God takes a text, and preacheth patience.

LXXIII

He that gets patience, and the blessing which
Preachers conclude with, hath not lost his pains.
He that by being at Church escapes the ditch
Which he might fall in by companions, gains.
  He that loves God's abode, and to combine
  With saints on earth, shall one day with them shine.

LXXIV

Jest not at preacher's language or expression:
How know'st thou but thy sinnes made him miscarrie?
Then turn thy faults and his into confession:
God sent him, whatsoe'er he be, O, tarry,
 And love him for his Master; his condition,
 Though it be ill, makes him no ill physician.

LXXV

None shall in Hell such bitter pangs endure
As those who mock at God's way of salvation:
Whom oil and balsames kill, what salve can cure?
They drink with greedinesse a full damnation.
 The Jews refused thunder, and we folly;
 Though God do hedge us in, yet who is holy?

LXXVI

Summe up at night what thou hast done by day,
And in the morning what thou hast to do;
Dresse and undresse thy soul; mark the decay
And growth of it; if with thy watch that too
 Be down, then winde up both: since we shall be
 Most surely judg'd, make thy accounts agree.

LXXVII

In brief, acquit thee bravely, play the man:
Look not on pleasures as they come, but go;
Deferre not the least vertue: life's poore span
Make not an ell by trifling in thy wo.
 If thou do ill, the joy fades, not the pains;
 If well, the pain doth fade, the joy remains.

III SUPERLIMINARE

Thou whom the former precepts have
Sprinkled, and taught how to behave
Thy self in Church, approach and taste
The Churche's mysticall repast.

AVOID, PROFANENESSE! COME NOT HERE:
NOTHING BUT HOLY, PURE, AND CLEARE,
OR THAT WHICH GRONETH TO BE SO,
MAY AT HIS PERILL FURTHER GO.

IV THE CHURCH

The Altar

A broken Altar, Lord, Thy servant reares,
Made of a heart, and cemented with teares,
    Whose parts are as Thy hand did frame;
    No workman's tool hath touch'd the same.
        A heart alone
        Is such a stone
        As nothing but
        Thy power doth cut.
        Wherefore each part
        Of my hard heart
        Meets in this frame,
        To praise Thy name:
That, if I chance to hold my peace,
These stones to praise Thee may not cease.
O, let Thy blessèd Sacrifice be mine,
And sanctifie this Altar to be Thine!

The Sacrifice

O all ye who passe by, whose eyes and minde
To worldly things are sharp, but to Me blinde –
To Me, Who took eyes that I might you finde:
        Was ever grief like Mine?

The princes of My people make a head
Against their Maker: they do wish Me dead,
Who cannot wish, except I give them bread:
        Was ever grief like Mine?

Without Me, each one who doth now Me brave
Had to this day been an Egyptian slave;
They use that power against Me which I gave:
        Was ever grief like Mine?

Mine own Apostle who the bag did beare,
Though he had all I had, did not forbeare
To sell Me also, and to put Me there:
        Was ever grief like Mine?

For thirtie pence he did My death devise
Who at three hundred did the ointment prize,
Not half so sweet as My sweet sacrifice:
        Was ever grief like Mine?

Therefore My soul melts, and My Heart's deare treasure
Drops bloud, the only beads My words to measure:
Oh, let this cup passe, if it be Thy pleasure:
        Was ever grief like Mine?

These drops being temper'd with a sinner's tears,
A balsome are for both the hemispheres,
Curing all wounds but mine, all but My fears:
        Was ever grief like Mine?

Yet My disciples sleep; I cannot gain
One houre of watching; but their drowsie brain
Comforts not Me, and doth My doctrine stain:
        Was ever grief like Mine?

'Arise! arise! they come!' Look how they runne!
Alas, what haste they make to be undone!
How with their lanterns do they seek the sunne!
       Was ever grief like Mine?

With clubs and staves they seek Me as a thief,
Who am the way of truth, the true relief,
Most true to those who are My greatest grief:
       Was ever grief like Mine?

Judas, dost thou betray Me with a kisse?
Canst thou finde hell about My lips, and misse
Of life just at the gates of life and blisse?
       Was ever grief like Mine?

See, they lay hold on Me, not with the hands
Of faith, but furie; yet at their commands;
I suffer binding, Who have loos'd their bands:
       Was ever grief like Mine?

All My disciples flie; fear puts a barre
Betwixt My friends and Me: they leave the starre
That brought the wise men of the East from farre:
       Was ever grief like Mine?

Then from one ruler to another, bound
They leade Me, urging that it was not sound
What I taught; comments would the text confound:
       Was ever grief like Mine?

The Priest and rulers all false witnesse seek
'Gainst Him Who seeks not life, but is the meek
And readie Paschal Lambe of this great week:
       Was ever grief like Mine?

Then they accuse Me of great blasphemie,
That I did thrust into the Deitie,
Who never thought that any robberie:
       Was ever grief like Mine?

Some said that I the Temple to the floore
In three days raz'd, and raisèd as before:
Why, He that built the world can do much more:
      Was ever grief like Mine?

Then they condemne Me all, with that same breath
Which I do give them daily, unto death;
Thus Adam my first breathing rendereth:
      Was ever grief like Mine?

They binde and leade Me unto Herod; he
Sends Me to Pilate: this makes them agree;
But yet their friendship is My enmitie:
      Was ever grief like Mine?

Herod and all his bands do set Me light,
Who teach all hands to warre, fingers to fight,
And onely am the Lord of hosts and might:
      Was ever grief like Mine?

Herod in judgement sits, while I do stand,
Examines Me with a censorious hand;
I him obey, Who all things else command:
      Was ever grief like Mine?

The Jews accuse Me with despitefulnesse,
And, vying malice with My gentlenesse,
Pick quarrels with their onely happinesse:
      Was ever grief like Mine?

I answer nothing, but with patience prove
If stony hearts will melt with gentle love:
But who does hawk at eagles with a dove?
      Was ever grief like Mine?

My silence rather doth augment their crie;
My dove doth back into My bosome flie,
Because the raging waters still are high:
      Was ever grief like Mine?

Hark how they crie aloud still, Crucifie!
It is not fit He live a day! they crie,
Who cannot live lesse then eternally:
    Was ever grief like Mine?

Pilate, a stranger, holdeth off; but they,
Mine own deare people, cry, Away, away!
With noises confusèd frighting the day:
    Was ever grief like Mine?

Yet still they shout, and crie, and stop their eares,
Putting My life among their sinnes and fears,
And therefore wish my bloud on them and theirs:
    Was ever grief like Mine?

See how spite cankers things! – these words, aright
Usèd and wishèd, are the whole world's light;
But hony is their gall, brightnesse their night:
    Was ever grief like Mine?

They choose a murderer, and all agree
In him to do themselves a courtesie;
For it was their own cause who killèd Me:
    Was ever grief like Mine?

And a seditious murderer he was;
But I the Prince of Peace, – peace that doth passe
All understanding more then heav'n doth glasse:
    Was ever grief like Mine?

Why, Cesar is their onely king, not I.
He clave the stonie rock when they were drie,
But surely not their hearts, as I well trie:
    Was ever grief like Mine?

Ah, how they scourge Me! yet my tendernesse
Doubles each lash: and yet their bitternesse
Windes up My grief to a mysteriousnesse:
    Was ever grief like Mine?

They buffet Me and box Me as they list,
Who grasp the earth and heaven with My fist,
And never yet whom I would punish miss'd:
        Was ever grief like Mine?

Behold, they spit on Me in scornfull wise,
Who by My spittle gave the blinde man eies,
Leaving his blindnesse to Mine enemies:
        Was ever grief like Mine?

My face they cover, though it be divine:
As Moses' face was vailèd, so is Mine,
Lest on their double-dark souls either shine:
        Was ever grief like Mine?

Servants and abjects flout Me, they are wittie;
'Now prophesie who strikes Thee,' is their dittie;
So they in Me denie themselves all pitie:
        Was ever grief like Mine?

And now I am deliver'd unto death;
Which each one calls for so with utmost breath,
That he before Me well-nigh suffereth:
        Was ever grief like Mine?

Weep not, deare friends, since I for both have wept
When all My tears were bloud, the while you slept:
Your tears for your own fortunes should be kept:
        Was ever grief like Mine?

The souldiers lead Me to the common-hall:
There they deride Me, they abuse Me all;
Yet for twelve heav'nly legions I could call:
        Was ever grief like Mine?

Then with a scarlet robe they Me aray,
Which shews My bloud to be the onely way,
And cordiall left to repair man's decay:
        Was ever grief like Mine?

Then on My head a crown of thorns I wear;
For these are all the grapes Sion doth bear,
Though I My vine planted and watrèd there:
      Was ever grief like Mine?

So sits the Earth's great curse in Adam's fall
Upon My head; so I remove it all
From th' earth unto My brows, and bear the thrall:
      Was ever grief like Mine?

Then with the reed they gave to Me before
They strike My head, the rock from whence all store
Of heav'nly blessings issue evermore:
      Was ever grief like Mine?

They bow their knees to Me, and cry, 'Hail, King!'
What ever scoffes or scornfulnesse can bring,
I am the floore, the sink, where they it fling:
      Was ever grief like Mine?

Yet since man's scepters are as frail as reeds,
And thorny all their crowns, bloudie their weeds,
I, Who am Truth, turn into truth their deeds:
      Was ever grief like Mine?

The souldiers also spit upon that Face
Which angels did desire to have the grace,
And prophets, once to see, but found no place:
      Was ever grief like Mine?

Thus trimmèd forth they bring Me to the rout,
Who 'Crucifie Him!' crie with one strong shout.
God holds His peace at man, and man cries out:
      Was ever grief like Mine?

They leade Me in once more, and putting then
Mine own clothes on, they leade Me out agen.
Whom devils flie, thus is He toss'd of men:
      Was ever grief like Mine?

And now wearie of sport, glad to ingrosse
All spite in one, counting My life their losse,
They carrie Me to My most bitter crosse:
        Was ever grief like Mine?

My crosse I bear My self, untill I faint:
Then Simon bears it for Me by constraint, –
The decreed burden of each mortal saint:
        Was ever grief like Mine?

O, all ye who passe by, behold and see:
Man stole the fruit, but I must climbe the tree, –
The tree of life to all but onely Me:
        Was ever grief like Mine?

Lo, here I hang, charg'd with a world of sinne,
The greater world o' th' two; for that came in
By words, but this by sorrow I must win:
        Was ever grief like Mine?

Such sorrow as if sinfull man could feel,
Or feel his part, he would not cease to kneel
Till all were melted, though he were all steel:
        Was ever grief like Mine?

But, O My God, My God, why leav'st Thou Me,
The Sonne in Whom Thou dost delight to be?
My God, My God –
        Never was grief like Mine.

Shame tears My soul, My bodie many a wound;
Sharp nails pierce this, but sharper that confound, –
Reproches which are free, while I am bound:
        Was ever grief like Mine?

'Now heal Thyself, Physician; now come down.'
Alas, I did so, when I left My crown
And Father's smile for you, to feel His frown:
        Was ever grief like Mine?

In healing not Myself there doth consist
All that salvation which ye now resist;
Your safetie in My sicknesse doth subsist:
        Was ever grief like Mine?

Betwixt two theeves I spend My utmost breath,
As he that for some robberie suffereth:
Alas, what have I stollen from you? death:
        Was ever grief like Mine?

A king My title is, prefixt on high;
Yet by My subjects am condemn'd to die
A servile death in servile companie:
        Was ever grief like Mine?

They gave Me vinegar mingled with gall,
But more with malice: yet, when they did call,
With manna, angels' food, I fed them all:
        Was ever grief like Mine?

They part My garments, and by lot dispose
My coat, the type of love, which once cur'd those
Who sought for help, never malicious foes:
        Was ever grief like Mine?

Nay, after death their spite shall further go;
For they will pierce My side, I full well know;
That as sinne came, so Sacraments might flow:
        Was ever grief like Mine?

But now I die; now all is finishèd;
My wo man's weal, and now I bow My head:
Onely let others say, when I am dead,
        Never was grief like Mine.

The Thanksgiving

Oh King of grief – a title strange, yet true,
    To Thee of all kings onely due –
Oh King of wounds, how shall I grieve for Thee,
    Who in all grief preventest me?
Shall I weep bloud? why, Thou hast wept such store,
    That all Thy body was one doore.
Shall I be scourgèd, flouted, boxèd, sold?
    'Tis but to tell the tale is told.
'My God, My God, why dost Thou part from Me?'
    Was such a grief as cannot be.
Shall I, then, sing, skipping Thy dolefull storie,
    And side with Thy triumphant glorie?
Shall Thy strokes be my stroking? thorns my flower?
    Thy rod my posie? crosse my bower?
But how, then, shall I imitate Thee, and
    Copie Thy fair though bloudie hand?
Surely I will revenge me on Thy love,
    And trie who shall victorious prove.
If Thou dost give me wealth, I will restore
    All back unto Thee by the poore.
If Thou dost give me honour, men shall see
    The honour doth belong to Thee.
I will not marry; or, if she be mine,
    She and her children shall be Thine.
My bosome-friend, if he blaspheme Thy name,
    I will tear thence his love and fame.
One half of me being gone, the rest I give
    Unto some chapell, die or live.
As for Thy passion – But of that anon,
    When with the other I have done.
For Thy predestination, I'le contrive
    That three years hence, if I survive,
I'le build a spittle, or mend common wayes,
    But mend mine own without delayes.
Then I will use the works of Thy creation,
    As if I us'd them but for fashion.
The world and I will quarrell; and the yeare
    Shall not perceive that I am here.

My musick shall find Thee, and ev'ry string
    Shall have his attribute to sing;
That all together may accord in Thee,
    And prove one God, one harmonie.
If Thou shalt give me wit, it shall appeare,
    If Thou hast giv'n it me, 'tis here.
Nay, I will reade Thy Booke, and never move
Till I have found therein Thy love,
Thy art of love, which I'le turn back on Thee:
O my deare Saviour, Victorie!
Then for Thy passion; I will do for that –
Alas, my God, I know not what.

The Reprisall

    I have consider'd it, and finde
There is no dealing with Thy mighty Passion;
For though I die for Thee, I am behinde;
    My sinnes deserve the condemnation.

    O, make me innocent, that I
May give a disentangled state and free;
And yet Thy wounds still my attempts defie,
    For by Thy death I die for Thee.

    Ah, was it not enough that Thou
By Thy eternall glorie didst outgo me?
Couldst Thou not Grief's sad conquests me allow,
    But in all vict'ries overthrow me?

    Yet by confession will I come
Into the conquest. Though I can do nought
Against Thee, in Thee I will overcome
    The man who once against Thee fought.

The Agonie

Philosophers have measur'd mountains,
Fathom'd the depths of seas, of states, and kings;
Walk'd with a staffe to heav'n, and tracèd fountains:
    But there are two vast, spacious things,
The which to measure it doth more behove;
Yet few there are that sound them, – Sinne and Love.

    Who would know Sinne, let him repair
Unto Mount Olivet; there shall he see
A Man so wrung with pains, that all His hair,
    His skinne, His garments bloudie be.
Sinne is that presse and vice, which forceth pain
To hunt his cruell food through ev'ry vein.

    Who knows not Love, let him assay
And taste that juice which, on the crosse, a pike
Did set again abroach; then let him say
    If ever he did taste the like.
Love is that liquor sweet and most divine,
Which my God feels as bloud, but I as wine.

The Sinner

Lord, how I am all ague when I seek
    What I have treasur'd in my memorie!
Since, if my soul make even with the week,
    Each seventh note by right is due to Thee.

I finde there quarries of pil'd vanities,
    But shreds of holinesse, that dare not venture
To shew their face, since crosse to Thy decrees:
    There the circumference earth is, heav'n the centre.

In so much dregs the quintessence is small;
    The spirit and good extract of my heart
    Comes to about the many hundredth part.
Yet, Lord, restore Thine image; heare my call;
    And though my hard heart scarce to Thee can grone,
    Remember that Thou once didst write in stone.

Good-Friday

O my chief good,
How shall I measure out Thy bloud?
How shall I count what Thee befell,
    And each grief tell?

Shall I Thy woes
Number according to Thy foes?
Or, since one starre show'd Thy first breath,
    Shall all Thy death?

Or shall each leaf
Which falls in Autumne score a grief?
Or cannot leaves, but fruit, be signe
    Of the True Vine?

Then let each houre
Of my whole life one grief devoure,
That Thy distresse through all may runne,
    And be my sunne.

Or rather let
My sev'rall sinnes their sorrows get,
That as each beast his cure doth know,
    Each sinne may so.

Since bloud is fittest, Lord, to write
Thy sorrows in and bloudie fight,
My heart hath store, write there, where in
One box doth lie both ink and sinne:

That when Sinne spies so many foes,
Thy whips, Thy nails, Thy wounds, Thy woes,
All come to lodge there, Sinne may say,
'No room for me,' and flie away.

Sinne being gone, O, fill the place,
And keep possession with Thy grace;
Lest sinne take courage, and return,
And all the writings blot or burn.

Redemption

Having been tenant long to a rich Lord,
   Not thriving, I resolvèd to be bold,
And make a suit unto Him, to afford
   A new small-rented lease, and cancell th' old.

In heaven at His manour I Him sought:
   They told me there, that He was lately gone
About some land, which he had dearly bought
   Long since on Earth, to take possession.

I straight return'd, and knowing His great birth,
   Sought Him accordingly in great resorts –
In cities, theatres, gardens, parks, and courts:
At length I heard a ragged noise and mirth

   Of theeves and murderers; there I Him espied,
Who straight, 'Your suit is granted,' said, and died.

Sepulchre

O blessed bodie, whither art Thou thrown?
No lodging for Thee but a cold hard stone!
So many hearts on earth, and yet not one
                   Receive Thee!

Sure there is room within our hearts good store,
For they can lodge transgressions by the score;
Thousands of toyes dwell there, yet out of doore
                   They leave Thee.

But that which shews them large shews them unfit.
Whatever sinne did this pure rock commit
Which holds Thee now? who have indited it
                   Of murder?

Where our hard hearts have took up stones to brain Thee,
And, missing this, most falsely did arraigne Thee,
Onely these stones in quiet entertain Thee,
                   And order.

And as of old the Law by heav'nly art
Was writ in stone; so Thou, which also art
The letter of the Word, find'st no fit heart
                To hold Thee.

Yet do we still persist as we began,
And so should perish, but that nothing can,
Though it be cold, hard, foul, from loving man
                Withhold Thee.

Easter

Rise, heart, Thy Lord is risen; sing His praise
                Without delayes,
Who takes thee by the hand, that thou likewise
                With Him mayst rise;
That, as His death calcinèd thee to dust,
His life may make thee gold, and, much more, just.

Awake, my lute, and struggle for thy part
                With all thy art:
The crosse taught all wood to resound His name
                Who bore the same;
His stretchèd sinews taught all strings what key
Is best to celebrate this most high day.

Consort both heart and lute, and twist a song
                Pleasant and long;
Or, since all musick is but three parts vied
                And multiplied,
O, let Thy blessèd Spirit bear a part,
And make up our defects with His sweet art.

The Song

    I got me flowers to straw Thy way,
    I got me boughs off many a tree;
    But Thou wast up by break of day,
    And brought'st Thy sweets along with Thee.

The sunne arising in the East,
Though he give light, and th' East perfume,
If they should offer to contest
With Thy arising, they presume.

Can there be any day but this,
Though many sunnes to shine endeavour?
We count three hundred, but we misse:
There is but one, and that one ever.

Another version, from the Williams MS.

I had preparèd many a flowre
To strow Thy way and victorie;
But Thou wast vp before myne houre,
Bringing Thy sweets along with Thee.

The sunn arising in the East,
Though hee bring light and th' other sents,
Can not make vp so braue a feast
As Thy discouerie presents.

Yet though my flours be lost, they say
A hart can never come too late;
Teach it to sing Thy praise this day,
And then this day my life shall date.

Easter Wings

Lord, Who createdst man in wealth and store,
  Though foolishly he lost the same,
    Decaying more and more,
      Till he became
        Most poore:

        With Thee
      O let me rise,
    As larks, harmoniously,
  And sing this day Thy victories:
Then shall the fall further the flight in me.

My tender age in sorrow did beginne;
  And still with sicknesses and shame
    Thou didst so punish sinne,
      That I became
        Most thinne.

        With Thee
      Let me combine,
    And feel this day Thy victorie;
  For, if I imp my wing on Thine,
Affliction shall advance the flight in me.

Holy Baptisme

As he that sees a dark and shadie grove
  Stayes not, but looks beyond it on the skie;
So, when I view my sinnes, mine eyes remove
  More backward still, and to that water flie

Which is above the heav'ns, whose spring and rent
  Is in my dear Redeemer's piercèd side.
O blessèd streams, either ye do prevent
  And stop our sinnes from growing thick and wide,

Or else give tears to drown them, as they grow.
In you Redemption measures all my time,
And spreads the plaister equall to the crime:
You taught the Book of Life my name, that so,

Whatever future sinnes should me miscall,
Your first acquaintance might discredit all.

Holy Baptisme

Since, Lord, to Thee
A narrow way and little gate
Is all the passage, on my infancie
Thou didst lay hold, and antedate
My faith in me.

O, let me still
Write Thee 'great God,' and me 'a childe';
Let me be soft and supple to Thy will,
Small to myself, to others milde,
Behither ill.

Although by stealth
My flesh get on; yet let her sister,
My soul, bid nothing, but preserve her wealth:
The growth of flesh is but a blister;
Childhood is health.

Nature

Full of rebellion, I would die,
Or fight, or travell, or denie
That Thou hast ought to do with me:
                    O, tame my heart;
                    It is Thy highest art
To captivate strongholds to Thee.

If Thou shalt let this venome lurk,
And in suggestions fume and work,
My soul will turn to bubbles straight,
      And thence, by kinde,
      Vanish into a winde,
Making Thy workmanship deceit.

O, smooth my rugged heart, and there
Engrave Thy rev'rend Law and fear;
Or make a new one, since the old
      If saplesse grown,
      And a much fitter stone
To hide my dust then Thee to hold.

Sinne

Lord, with what care hast Thou begirt us round!
 Parents first season us; then schoolmasters
Deliver us to laws; they send us, bound
 To rules of reason, holy messengers,

Pulpits and Sundayes, sorrow dogging sinne,
 Afflictions sorted, anguish of all sizes,
Fine nets and stratagems to catch us in,
 Bibles laid open, millions of surprises;

Blessings beforehand, tyes of gratefulnesse,
 The sound of glorie ringing in our eares,
Without, our shame; within, our consciences;
 Angels and grace, eternall hopes and fears.

Yet all these fences and their whole aray
One cunning bosome-sinne blows quite away.

Affliction

When first Thou didst entice to Thee my heart,
        I thought the service brave:
So many joyes I writ down for my part,
        Besides what I might have
Out of my stock of naturall delights,
Augmented with Thy gracious benefits.

I lookèd on Thy furniture so fine,
        And made it fine to me;
Thy glorious houshold-stuffe did me entwine,
        And 'tice me unto Thee;
Such starres I counted mine: both heav'n and earth
Payd me my wages in a world of mirth.

What pleasures could I want, whose King I served,
        Where joyes my fellows were?
Thus argu'd into hopes, my thoughts reserved
        No place for grief or fear;
Therefore my sudden soul caught at the place,
And made her youth and fiercenesse seek Thy face.

At first thou gav'st me milk and sweetnesses,
        I had my wish and way;
My days were straw'd with flow'rs and happinesses;
        There was no moneth but May.
But with my yeares sorrow did twist and grow,
And made a partie unawares for wo.

My flesh began unto my soul in pain,
        Sicknesses cleave my bones,
Consuming agues dwell in ev'ry vein,
        And tune my breath to grones:
Sorrow was all my soul; I scarce beleeved,
Till grief did tell me roundly, that I lived.

When I got health, Thou took'st away my life,
        And more, – for my friends die:
My mirth and edge was lost, a blunted knife
        Was of more use then I:

Thus thinne and lean, without a fence or friend,
I was blown through with ev'ry storm and winde.

Whereas my birth and spirit rather took
                    The way that takes the town,
Thou didst betray me to a lingring book,
                    And wrap me in a gown;
I was entangled in the world of strife
Before I had the power to change my life.

Yet, for I threatned oft the siege to raise,
                    Not simpring all mine age,
Thou often didst with academick praise
                    Melt and dissolve my rage:
I took Thy sweetened pill till I came neare;
I could not go away, nor persevere.

Yet lest perchance I should too happie be
                    In my unhappinesse,
Turning my purge to food, Thou throwest me
                    Into more sicknesses:
Thus doth Thy power cross-bias me, not making
Thine own gift good, yet me from my ways taking.

Now I am here, what Thou wilt do with me
                    None of my books will show:
I reade, and sigh, and wish I were a tree, –
                    For sure then I should grow
To fruit or shade; at least some bird would trust
Her houshold to me, and I should be just.

Yet, though Thou troublest me, I must be meek;
                    In weaknesse must be stout.
Well, I will change the service, and go seek
                    Some other master out.
Ah, my deare God, though I am clean forgot,
Let me not love Thee, if I love Thee not.

Repentance

Lord, I confesse my sin is great;
  Great is my sinne: O, gently treat
With Thy quick flow'r Thy momentanie bloom,
   Whose life still pressing
   Is one undressing,
  A steadie aiming at a tombe.

Man's age is two houres' work, or three;
  Each day doth round about us see.
Thus are we to delights, but we are all
   To sorrows old,
   If life be told
From what life feeleth, Adam's fall.

O, let Thy height of mercie, then,
  Compassionate short-breathèd men;
Cut me not off for my most foul transgression
   I do confesse
   My foolishnesse;
My God, accept of my confession.

Sweeten at length this bitter bowl
  Which Thou hast pour'd into my soul;
Thy wormwood turn to health, windes to fair weather:
   For if Thou stay,
   I and this day,
As we did rise, we die together.

When Thou for sinne rebukest man,
  Forthwith he waxeth wo and wan;
Bitternesse fills our bowels, all our hearts
   Pine and decay
   And drop away,
And carrie with them th' other parts.

But Thou wilt sinne and grief destroy;
  That so the broken bones may joy,
And tune together in a well-set song,
   Full of His praises
   Who dead men raises.
Fractures well cur'd make us more strong.

Faith

Lord, how couldst Thou so much appease
Thy wrath for sinne, as when man's sight was dimme
And could see little, to regard his ease,
    And bring by faith all things to him?

Hungrie I was, and had no meat:
I did conceit a most delicious feast, –
I had it straight, and did as truly eat
    As ever did a welcome guest.

There is a rare outlandish root,
Which when I could not get, I thought it here;
That apprehension cur'd so well my foot,
    That I can walk to heav'n well neare.

I owèd thousands, and much more;
I did beleeve that I did nothing owe,
And liv'd accordingly; my creditor
    Beleeves so too, and lets me go.

Faith makes me any-thing, or all
That I beleeve is in the sacred storie;
And where sinne placeth me in Adam's fall,
    Faith sets me higher in his glorie.

If I go lower in the book,
What can be lower then the common manger?
Faith puts me there with Him Who sweetly took
    Our flesh and frailtie, death and danger.

If blisse had lien in art or strength,
None but the wise or strong had gainèd it;
Where now by faith all arms are of a length,
    One size doth all conditions fit.

A peasant may beleeve as much
As a great clerk, and reach the highest stature:
Thus dost Thou make proud knowledge bend and crouch,
    While grace fills up uneven nature.

When creatures had no reall light
Inherent in them, Thou didst make the sunne
Impute a lustre, and allow them bright,
    And in this shew what Christ hath done.

That which before was darkned clean
With bushie groves, pricking the looker's eie,
Vanisht away when Faith did change the scene;
    And then appear'd a glorious skie.

What though my bodie runne to dust?
Faith cleaves unto it, counting ev'ry grain
With an exact and most particular trust,
    Reserving all for flesh again.

Prayer

Prayer, the Churche's banquet, Angels' age,
    God's breath in man returning to his birth,
The soul in paraphrase, heart in pilgrimage,
    The Christian plummet sounding heav'n and earth;

Engine against th' Almightie, sinner's towre,
    Reversèd thunder, Christ-side-piercing spear,
The six-daies-world transposing in an houre,
    A kinde of tune which all things heare and fear;

Softnesse, and peace, and joy, and love, and blisse,
    Exalted manna, gladnesse of the best,
    Heaven in ordinarie, man well drest,
The milkie way, the bird of Paradise,

    Church-bels beyond the stars heard, the soul's bloud,
    The land of spices, something understood.

The Holy Communion

Not in rich furniture or fine aray,
    Nor in a wedge of gold,
    Thou, Who from me wast sold,
  To me dost now Thyself convey;
For so Thou shouldst without me still have been,
    Leaving within me sinne:

But by the way of nourishment and strength,
    Thou creep'st into my breast;
    Making Thy way my rest,
  And Thy small quantities my length,
Which spread their forces into every part,
    Meeting Sinne's force and art.

Yet can these not get over to my soul,
    Leaping the wall that parts
    Our souls and fleshy hearts;
  But as th' outworks, they may controll
My rebel flesh, and, carrying Thy name,
    Affright both sinne and shame.

Onely Thy grace, which with these elements comes,
    Knoweth the ready way,
    And hath the privie key,
  Op'ning the soul's most subtile rooms;
While those, to spirits refin'd, at doore attend
    Dispatches from their friend.

Give me my captive soul, or take
    My bodie also thither.
Another lift like this will make
    Them both to be together.

Before that sinne turn'd flesh to stone,
    And all our lump to leaven,
A fervent sigh might well have blown
    Our innocent earth to heaven.

For sure when Adam did not know
    To sinne, or sinne to smother,
He might to heav'n from Paradise go,
    As from one room t' another.

Thou hast restor'd us to this ease
    By this Thy heav'nly bloud,
Which I can go to when I please,
    And leave th' earth to their food.

Antiphon

Cho.   Let all the world in ev'ry corner sing
              My God and King.
Vers.   The heav'ns are not too high,
        His praise may thither flye;
        The earth is not too low,
        His praises there may grow.
Cho.   Let all the world in ev'ry corner sing
              My God and King.
Vers.   The Church with psalms must shout,
        No door can keep them out:
        But above all, the heart
        Must bear the longest part.
Cho.   Let all the world in ev'ry corner sing
              My God and King.

Love

I

Immortal love, author of this great frame,
   Sprung from that beauty which can never fade,
How hath man parcel'd out Thy glorious name,
   And thrown it on that dust which Thou hast made,

While mortall love doth all the title gain!
   Which siding with Invention, they together
Bear all the sway, possessing heart and brain –
   Thy workmanship – and give Thee share in neither.

Wit fancies beautie, beautie raiseth wit;
   The world is theirs, they two play out the game,
   Thou standing by: and though Thy glorious name
Wrought our deliverance from th' infernall pit,

   Who sings Thy praise ? Onely a skarf or glove
   Doth warm our hands, and make them write of love.

II

Immortall Heat, O let Thy greater flame
   Attract the lesser to it; let those fires
Which shall consume the world first make it tame,
   And kindle in our hearts such true desires

As may consume our lusts, and make Thee way:
   Then shall our hearts pant Thee, then shall our brain
All her invention on Thine altar lay,
   And there in hymnes send back Thy fire again.

Our eies shall see Thee, which before saw dust –
   Dust blown by Wit, till that they both were blinde:
   Thou shalt recover all Thy goods in kinde,
Who wert disseizèd by usurping lust:

   All knees shall bow to Thee; all wits shall rise,
   And praise Him Who did make and mend our eies.

The Temper

How should I praise Thee, Lord? how should my rymes
    Gladly engrave Thy love in steel,
    If, what my soul doth feel sometimes,
        My soul might ever feel!

Although there were some fourtie heav'ns or more,
    Sometimes I peere above them all;
    Sometimes I hardly reach a score,
        Sometimes to Hell I fall.

O, rack me not to such a vast extent,
    Those distances belong to Thee;
    The world's too little for Thy tent,
        A grave too big for me.

Wilt Thou meet arms with man, that Thou dost stretch
    A crumme of dust from heav'n to hell?
    Will great God measure with a wretch?
        Shall he Thy stature spell?

O, let me, when Thy roof my soul hath hid,
    O, let me roost and nestle there;
    Then of a sinner Thou art rid,
        And I of hope and fear.

Yet take Thy way; for sure Thy way is best:
    Stretch or contract me, Thy poore debter;
    This is but tuning of my breast,
        To make the musick better.

Whether I flie with angels, fall with dust,
    Thy hands made both, and I am there;
    Thy power and love, my love and trust,
        Make one place ev'rywhere.

The Temper

It cannot be: where is that mightie joy
    Which just now took up all my heart?
    Lord, if Thou must needs use Thy dart,
Save that and me, or sin for both destroy.

The grosser world stands to Thy word and art;
    But Thy diviner world of grace
    Thou suddenly dost raise and race,
And every day a new Creatour art.

O, fix Thy chair of grace, that all my powers
    May also fix their reverence;
    For when Thou dost depart from hence,
They grow unruly, and sit in Thy bowers.

Scatter or binde them all to bend to Thee;
    Though elements change, and heaven move,
    Let not Thy higher Court remove,
But keep a standing Majestie in me

Jordan

Who says that fictions onely and false hair
Become a verse? Is there in truth no beautie?
Is all good structure in a winding-stair?
May no lines passe, except they do their dutie
    Not to a true, but painted chair?

Is it no verse, except enchanted groves
And sudden arbours shadow coarse-spunne lines?
Must purling streams refresh a lover's loves?
Must all be vail'd while he that reades divines,
    Catching the sense at two removes?

Shepherds are honest people, let them sing:
Riddle who list, for me, and pull for prime,
I envie no man's nightingale or spring;
Nor let them punish me with loss of rhyme,
    Who plainly say, My God, my King.

Employment

If, as a flowre doth spread and die,
    Thou wouldst extend me to some good,
Before I were by frost's extremitie
       Nipt in the bud;

The sweetnesse and the praise were Thine,
    But the extension and the room
Which in Thy garland I should fill were mine
       At Thy great doom.

For as Thou dost impart Thy grace,
    The greater shall our glorie be;
The measure of our joyes is in this place,
       The stuffe with Thee.

Let me not languish, then, and spend
    A life as barren to Thy praise
As is the dust to which that life doth tend,
       But with delaies.

All things are busie; onely I
    Neither bring hony with the bees,
Nor flowres to make that, nor the husbandrie
       To water these.

I am no link of Thy great chain,
    But all my companie is a weed.
Lord, place me in Thy consort; give one strain
       To my poore reed.

The Holy Scriptures

I

Oh book! infinite sweetnesse! let my heart
    Suck ev'ry letter, and a hony gain
Precious for any grief in any part,
    To cleare the breast, to mollifie all pain.

Thou art all health, health thriving till it make
    A full eternitie; thou art a masse
Of strange delights, where we may wish and take.
    Ladies, look here; this is the thankfull glasse,

That mends the looker's eyes; this is the well
    That washes what it shows. Who can indeare
    Thy praise too much? thou art heaven's Lidger here,
Working against the States of death and hell.

    Thou art Joye's handsell; heav'n lies flat in thee
    Subject to ev'ry mounter's bended knee.

II

Oh that I knew how all thy lights combine,
    And the configurations of their glorie!
Seeing not onely how each verse doth shine,
    But all the constellations of the storie.

This verse marks that, and both do make a motion
    Unto a third, that ten leaves off doth lie:
Then as dispersèd herbs do watch a potion,
    These three make up some Christian's destinie.

Such are thy secrets, which my life makes good,
    And comments on thee: for in ev'ry thing
    Thy words do finde me out, and parallels bring,
And in another make me understood.

    Starres are poore books, and oftentimes do misse;
    This book of starres lights to eternall blisse.

Whit Sunday

Listen, sweet Dove, unto my song,
And spread thy golden wings in me;
Hatching my tender heart so long,
Till it get wing, and flie away with Thee.

Where is that fire which once descended
On Thy Apostles? Thou didst then
Keep open house, richly attended,
Feasting all comers by twelve chosen men.

Such glorious gifts Thou didst bestow,
That th' earth did like a heav'n appeare:
The starres were coming down to know
If they might mend their wages, and serve here.

The sunne, which once did shine alone,
Hung down his head, and wisht for night,
When he beheld twelve sunnes for one
Going about the world and giving light.

But since those pipes of gold, which brought
That cordiall water to our ground,
Were cut and martyr'd by the fault
Of those who did themselves through their side wound,

Thou shutt'st the doore, and keep'st within;
Scarce a good joy creeps through the chink;
And if the braves of conqu'ring sinne
Did not excite Thee, we should wholly sink.

Lord, though we change, Thou art the same,
The same sweet God of love and light:
Restore this day, for Thy great name,
Unto his ancient and miraculous right.

Grace

My stock lies dead, and no increase
Doth my dull husbandrie improve:
O, let Thy graces, without cease
                 Drop from above!

If still the sunne should hide his face,
Thy house would but a dungeon prove,
Thy works, Night's captives: O, let grace
                 Drop from above!

The dew doth ev'ry morning fall;
And shall the dew out-strip Thy Dove, –
The dew, for which grasse cannot call,
                 Drop from above?

Death is still working like a mole,
And digs my grave at each remove;
Let grace work too, and on my soul
                 Drop from above.

Sinne is still hammering my heart
Unto a hardnesse void of love:
Let suppling grace, to crosse his art,
                 Drop from above.

O, come; for Thou dost know the way:
Or if to me Thou wilt not move,
Remove me where I need not say,
                 Drop from above.

Praise

To write a verse or two is all the praise
        That I can raise:
Mend my estate in any wayes,
        Thou shalt have more.

I go to church: help me to wings, and I
        Will thither flie:
Or if I mount unto the skie,
        I will do more.

Man is all weaknesse; there is no such thing
        As prince or king:
His arm is short; yet with a sling
        He may do more,

A herb distill'd and drunk may dwell next doore,
        On the same floore,
To a brave soul: exalt the poore,
        They can do more.

O, raise me, then: poore bees, that work all day,
        Sting my delay,
Who have a work as well as they,
        And much, much more.

Affliction

Kill me not ev'ry day,
Thou Lord of life; since Thy one death for me
Is more than all my deaths can be,
Though I in broken pay
Die over each houre of Methusalem's stay.

If all men's tears were let
Into one common sewer, sea, and brine,
What were they all compar'd to Thine?
Wherein, if they were set,
They would discolour Thy most bloudy sweat.

Thou art my grief alone,
Thou, Lord, conceal it not: and as Thou art
All my delight, so all my smart:
Thy crosse took up in one,
By way of imprest, all my future mone.

Mattens

I cannot ope mine eyes,
But Thou art ready there to catch
My morning soul and sacrifice:
Then we must needs for that day make a match.

My God, what is a heart?
Silver, or gold, or precious stone,
Or starre, or rainbow, or a part
Of all these things, or all of them in one?

My God, what is a heart,
That Thou shouldst it so eye and wooe,
Powring upon it all Thy art,
As if that Thou hadst nothing els to do?

Indeed, man's whole estate
Amounts, and richly, to serve Thee:
He did not heau'n and earth create,
Yet studies them, not Him by Whom they be.

Teach me Thy love to know;
That this new light, which now I see,
May both the work and workman show;
Then by a sunne-beam I will climb to Thee.

Sinne

O that I could sinne once see!
We paint the devil foul, yet he
Hath some good in him, all agree:
Sinne is sat opposite to th' Almighty, seeing
It wants the good of vertue and of being.

But God more care of us hath had;
If apparitions make us sad,
By eight of sinne we should grow mad.
Yet as in sleep we see foul death, and live,
So devils are our sinnes in perspective.

Even-Song

Blest be the God of love,
Who gave me eyes, and light, and power this day,
    Both to be busie and to play:
    But much more blest be God above,

    Who gave me sight alone,
    Which to Himself He did denie:
    For when He sees my waies, I die;
But I have got His Sonne, and He hath none.

    What have I brought thee home
For this Thy love? have I discharg'd the debt
    Which this daye's favour did beget?
    I ranne; but all I brought was fome.

    Thy diet, care, and cost
    Do end in bubbles, balls of winde;
    Of winde to Thee whom I have crost,
But balls of wilde-fire to my troubled minde,

    Yet still Thou goest on,
And now with darknesse closest wearie eyes,
    Saying to man, 'It doth suffice;
    Henceforth repose, your work is done.'

    Thus in Thy ebony box
    Thou dost inclose us, till the day
    Put our amendment in our way,
And give new wheels to our disorder'd clocks.

    I muse which shows more love,
The day or night; that is the gale, this th' harbour;
    That is the walk, and this the arbour;
    Or that the garden, this the grove.

    My God, Thou art all love:
    Not one poore minute 'scapes Thy breast,
    But brings a favour from above;
And in this love, more then in bed, I rest.

Church-Monuments

While that my soul repairs to her devotion,
Here I intombe my flesh, that it betimes
May take acquaintance of this heap of dust,
To which the blast of Death's incessant motion,
Fed with the exhalation of our crimes,
Drives all at last. Therefore I gladly trust

My bodie to this school, that it may learn
To spell his elements, and finde his birth
Written in dustie heraldrie and lines;
Which dissolution sure doth best discern,
Comparing dust with dust, and earth with earth.
These laugh at jeat and marble, put for signes,

To sever the good fellowship of dust,
And spoil the meeting: what shall point out them,
When they shall bow, and kneel, and fall down flat
To kisse those heaps which now they have in trust?
Deare flesh, while I do pray, learn here thy stemme
And true descent, that, when thou shalt grow fat,

And wanton in thy cravings, thou mayst know
That flesh is but the glasse which holds the dust
That measures all our time; which also shall
Be crumbled into dust. Mark here below
How tame these ashes are, how free from lust, –
That thou mayst fit thyself against thy fall.

Church Musick

Sweetest of sweets, I thank you: when displeasure
　　Did through my bodie wound my minde,
You took me thence, and in your house of pleasure
　　A daintie lodging me assign'd.

Now I in you without a bodie move,
　　Rising and falling with your wings;
We both together sweetly live and love,
　　Yet say sometimes, 'God help poore kings!'

Comfort, I'le die; for if you poste from me,
　　Sure I shall do so and much more;
But if I travell in your companie,
　　You know the way to heaven's doore.

Church Lock and Key

I know it is my sinne which locks Thine eares
　　And bindes Thy hands,
Out-crying my requests, drowning my tears,
Or else the chilnesse of my faint demands.

But as cold hands are angrie with the fire,
　　And mend it still,
So I do lay the want of my desire
Not on my sinnes, or coldnesse, but Thy will.

Yet heare, O God, onely for His bloud's sake,
　　Which pleads for me:
For though sinnes plead too, yet, like stones, they make
His bloud's sweet current much more loud to be.

The Church Floore

Mark you the floore? that square and speckled stone,
    Which looks so firm and strong,
        Is PATIENCE:

And th' other black and grave, wherewith each one
    Is checker'd all along,
        HUMILITIE:

The gentle rising, which on either hand
    Leads to the quire above,
        Is CONFIDENCE:

But the sweet cement, which in one sure band
    Ties the whole frame, is LOVE
        And CHARITIE.

        *

  Hither sometimes Sinne steals, and stains
  The marble's neat and curious veins;
But all is cleansèd when the marble weeps.
  Sometimes Death, puffing at the doore,
  Blows all the dust about the floore;
But while he thinks to spoil the room, he sweeps.

  Blest be the Architect Whose art
  Could build so strong in a weak heart!

The Windows

Lord, how can man preach Thy eternall word?
    He is a brittle crazie glasse;
Yet in Thy temple Thou dost him afford
    This glorious and transcendent place,
    To be a window through Thy grace.

But when Thou dost anneal in glasse Thy storie,
    Making Thy life to shine within
The holy preachers, then the light and glorie
    More rev'rend grows, and more doth win;
    Which else shows watrish, bleak, and thin.

Doctrine and life, colours and light, in one
    When they combine and mingle, bring
A strong regard and aw; but speech alone
    Doth vanish like a flaring thing,
    And in the eare, not conscience, ring.

Trinitie Sunday

Lord, Who hast form'd me out of mud,
  And hast redeem'd me through Thy bloud,
  And sanctifi'd me to do good.

Purge all my sinnes done heretofore;
  For I confesse my heavie score,
  And I will strive to sinne no more.

Enrich my heart, mouth, hands in me,
  With faith, with hope, with charitie,
  That I may runne, rise, rest with Thee.

Content

Peace, mutt'ring thoughts, and do not grudge to keep
    Within the walls of your own breast:
Who cannot on his own bed sweetly sleep,
    Can on another's hardly rest.

Gad not abroad at ev'ry quest and call
    Of an untrainèd hope or passion;
To court each place or fortune that doth fall
    Is wantonnesse in contemplation.

Mark how the fire in flints doth quiet lie,
    Content and warm t' it self alone;
But when it would appeare to others' eye,
    Without a knock it never shone.

Give me the pliant minde, whose gentle measure
    Complies and suites with all estates;
Which can let loose to a crown, and yet with pleasure
    Take up within a cloister's gates.

This soul doth span the world, and hang content
    From either pole unto the centre;
Where in each room of the well-furnisht tent
    He lies warm, and without adventure.

The brags of life are but a nine-dayes wonder;
    And after death the fumes that spring
From private bodies make as big a thunder
    As those which rise from a huge king.

Onely thy chronicle is lost: and yet
    Better by worms be all once spent
Then to have hellish moths still gnaw and fret
    Thy name in books which may not rent.

When all thy deeds, whose brunt thou feel'st alone,
    Are chaw'd by others' pens and tongue,
And as their wit is, their digestion,
    Thy nourisht fame is weak or strong,

Then cease discoursing, soul; till thine own ground;
   Do not thyself or friends importune:
He that by seeking hath himself once found,
   Hath ever found a happie fortune.

The Quidditie

   My God, a verse is not a crown,
   No point of honour, or gay suit,
   No hawk, or banquet, or renown,
   Nor a good sword, nor yet a lute.

   It cannot vault, or dance, or play,
   It never was in France or Spain,
   Nor can it entertain the day
   With a great stable or demain.

   It is no office, art, or news,
   Nor the Exchange or busie hall:
   But it is that which, while I use,
   I am with Thee: and 'MOST TAKE ALL.'

Humilitie

I saw the Vertues sitting hand in hand
In sev'rall ranks upon an azure throne,
Where all the beasts and fowls, by their command,
Presented tokens of submission:
Humilitie, who sat the lowest there,
      To execute their call,
When by the beasts the presents tendred were,
      Gave them about to all.

The angrie Lion did present his paw,
Which by consent was giv'n to Mansuetude;
The fearful Hare her eares, which by their law
Humilitie did reach to Fortitude;
The jealous Turkie brought his corall-chain,
      That went to Temperance;
On Justice was bestow'd the Foxe's brain,
      Kill'd in the way by chance.

At length the Crow, bringing the Peacock's plume –
For he would not – as they beheld the grace
Of that brave gift, each one began to fume,
And challenge it, as proper to his place,
Till they fell out; which when the beasts espied,
      They leapt upon the throne;
And if the Fox had liv'd to rule their side,
      They had depos'd each one.

Humilitie, who held the plume, at this
Did weep so fast, that the tears trickling down
Spoil'd all the train: then saying, 'Here it is
For which ye wrangle,' made them turn their frown
Against the beasts: so joyntly bandying,
      They drive them soon away;
And then amerc'd them, double gifts to bring
      At the next session-day.

Frailtie

Lord, in my silence how do I despise
      What upon trust
Is stylèd honour, riches, or fair eyes,
      But is fair dust!
  I surname them guilded clay,
  Deare earth, fine grasse or hay;
In all, I think my foot doth ever tread
      Upon their head.

But when I view abroad both regiments,
      The world's and Thine, –
Thine clad with simplenesse and sad events;
      The other fine,
  Full of glorie and gay weeds,
  Brave language, braver deeds, –
That which was dust before doth quickly rise,
      And prick mine eyes.

O, brook not this, lest if what even now
      My foot did tread
Affront those joyes wherewith Thou didst endow
      And long since wed
My poore soul, ev'n sick of love, –
It may a Babel prove,
Commodious to conquer heav'n and Thee,
      Planted in me.

Constancie

Who is the honest man?
He that doth still and strongly good pursue;
To God, his neighbour, and himself most true;
      Whom neither force nor fawning can
Unpinne, or wrench from giving all their due.

      Whose honestie is not
So loose or easie, that a ruffling winde
Can blow away, or glitt'ring look it blinde;
      Who rides his sure and even trot,
While the world now rides by, now lags behinde.

      Who, when great trials come,
Nor seeks nor shunnes them, but doth calmly stay,
Till he the thing and the example weigh:
      All being brought into a summe,
What place or person calls for he doth pay.

      Whom none can work or wooe
To use in any thing a trick or sleight,
For above all things he abhorres deceit;
      His words and works and fashion too
All of a piece, and all are cleare and straight.

      Who never melts or thaws
At close tentations: when the day is done,
His goodnesse sets not, but in dark can runne:
      The sunne to others writeth laws,
And is their vertue, Vertue is his sunne.

Who, when he is to treat
With sick folks, women, those whom passions sway,
Allows for that, and keeps his constant way;
        Whom others' faults do not defeat,
But though men fail him, yet his part doth play.

        Whom nothing can procure,
When the wide world runnes bias, from his will,
To writhe his limbs, and share, not mend, the ill.
        This is the Mark-man, safe and sure,
Who still is right, and prayes to be so still.

Affliction

My heart did heave, and there came forth 'O God!'
By that I knew that Thou wast in the grief,
To guide and govern it to my relief,
        Making a scepter of the rod:
        Hadst Thou not had Thy part,
Sure the unruly sigh had broke my heart.

But since Thy breath gave me both life and shape,
Thou know'st my tallies; and when there's assign'd
So much breath to a sigh, what's then behinde:
        Or if some yeares with it escape,
        The sigh then onely is
A gale to bring me sooner to my blisse.

Thy life on earth was grief, and Thou art still
Constant unto it, making it to be
A point of honour now to grieve in me,
        And in Thy members suffer ill.
        They who lament one crosse,
Thou dying daily, praise Thee to Thy losse.

The Starre

Bright spark, shot from a brighter place,
   Where beams surround my Saviour's face,
     Canst thou be any where
      So well as there?

Yet if thou wilt from thence depart,
   Take a bad lodging in my heart;
     For thou canst make a debter,
      And make it better.

First with thy fire-work burn to dust
   Folly, and worse then folly, lust:
     Then with thy light refine,
      And make it shine.

So, disengag'd from sinne and sicknesse,
   Touch it with thy celestial quicknesse,
     That it may hang and move
      After thy love.

Then with our trinitie, of light,
   Motion, and heat, let's take our flight
     Unto the place where thou
      Before did'st bow.

Get me a standing there, and place,
   Among the beams which crown the face
     Of Him Who dy'd to part
      Sinne and my heart;

That so among the rest I may
   Glitter, and curle, and winde as they:
     That winding is their fashion
      Of adoration.

Sure thou wilt joy by gaining me
   To flie home, like a laden bee
     Unto that hive of beams
      And garland-streams.

Sunday

O day most calm, most bright,
The fruit of this, the next world's bud,
Th' indorsement of supreme delight,
Writ by a friend, and with His bloud;
The couch of Time, Care's balm and bay:
The week were dark but for thy light;
   Thy torch doth show the way.

The other dayes and thou
Make up one man, whose face thou art,
Knocking at heaven with thy brow:
The worky-daies are the back-part;
The burden of the week lies there,
Making the whole to stoup and bow,
   Till thy release appeare.

Man had straight forward gone
To endlesse death; but thou dost pull
And turn us round to look on one
Whom, if we were not very dull,
We could not choose but look on still,
Since there is no place so alone
   The which He doth not fill.

Sundaies the pillars are
On which heav'n's palace archèd lies;
The other dayes fill up the spare
And hollow room with vanities:
They are the fruitfull beds and borders
In God's rich garden; that is bare
   Which parts their ranks and orders.

The Sundaies of man's life,
Thredded together on Time's string,
Make bracelets to adorn the wife
Of the eternall glorious King:
On Sunday heaven's gate stands ope;
Blessings are plentifull and rife,
   More plentifull then hope.

This day my Saviour rose,
And did inclose this light for His;
That, as each beast his manger knows,
Man might not of his fodder misse:
Christ hath took in this piece of ground,
And made a garden there for those
       Who want herbs for their wound.

       The rest of our creation
Our great Redeemer did remove
With the same shake which at His passion
Did th' earth and all things with it move.
As Samson bore the doores away,
Christ's hands, though nail'd, wrought our salvation,
       And did unhinge that day.

       The brightnesse of that day
We sullied by our foul offence:
Wherefore that robe we cast away,
Having a new at His expense,
Whose drops of bloud paid the full price
That was requir'd to make us gay,
       And fit for Paradise.

       Thou art a day of mirth:
And where the week-dayes trail on ground,
Thy flight is higher, as thy birth.
O, let me take thee at the bound,
Leaping with thee from sev'n to sev'n,
Till that we both, being toss'd from earth,
       Flie hand in hand to heav'n!

Avarice

Money, thou bane of blisse and source of wo,
    Whence com'st thou, that thou art so fresh and fine;
I know thy parentage is base and low, –
    Man found thee poore and dirtie in a mine.

Surely thou didst so little contribute
    To this great kingdome, which thou now hast got,
That he was fain, when thou wert destitute,
    To digge thee out of thy dark cave and grot.

Then forcing thee, by fire he made thee bright:
    Nay, thou hast got the face of man; for we
Have with our stamp and seal transferred our right;
    Thou art the man, and man but drosse to thee.

Man calleth thee his wealth, who made thee rich;
And while he digs out thee, falls in the ditch.

Ana[$^{Mary}_{Army}$]Gram

How well her name an 'Army' doth present,
In whom the 'Lord of Hosts' did pitch His tent!

To All Angels and Saints

Oh glorious spirits, who, after all your bands,
See the smooth face of God, without a frown
      Or strict commands;
Where ev'ry one is king, and hath his crown,
If not upon his head, yet in his hands;

Not out of envie or maliciousnesse
Do I forbear to crave your speciall aid:
      I would addresse
My vows to thee most gladly, blessèd Maid,
And Mother of my God, in my distresse:

Thou art the holy mine whence came the gold,
The great restorative for all decay
      In young and old;
Thou art the cabinet where the jewell lay,
Chiefly to thee would I my soul unfold.

But now, alas, I dare not; for our King,
Whom we do all joyntly adore and praise,
      Bids no such thing;
And where His pleasure no injunction layes –
'Tis your own case – ye never move a wing.

All worship is prerogative, and a flower
Of His rich crown from Whom lyes no appeal
      At the last houre:
Therefore we dare not from His garland steal,
To make a posie for inferiour power.

Although, then, others court you, if ye know
What's done on Earth, we shall not fare the worse
      Who do not so;
Since we are ever ready to disburse,
If any one our Master's hand can show.

Employment

He that is weary, let him sit;
   My soul would stirre
And trade in courtesies and wit,
   Quitting the furre
To cold complexions needing it.

Man is no starre, but a quick coal
   Of mortall fire:
Who blows it not, nor doth controll
   A faint desire,
Lets his own ashes choke his soul.

When th' elements did for place contest
   With Him Whose will
Ordain'd the highest to be best,
   The earth sate still,
And by the others is opprest.

Life is a businesse, not good-cheer;
   Ever in warres.
The sunne still shineth there or here,
   Whereas the starres
Watch an advantage to appeare.

Oh that I were an orenge-tree,
   That busie plant!
Then should I ever laden be,
   And never want
Some fruit for him that dressèd me.

But we are still too young or old;
   The man is gone
Before we do our wares unfold;
   So we freeze on,
Until the grave increase our cold.

Deniall

When my devotions could not pierce
      Thy silent eares,
Then was my heart broken, as was my verse;
      My breast was full of fears
         And disorder;

My bent thoughts, like a brittle bow,
      Did flie asunder;
Each took his way; some would to pleasures go,
      Some to the warres and thunder
         Of alarms.

As good go any where, they say,
      As to benumme
Both knees and heart in crying night and day,
      'Come, come, my God, O come!'
         But no hearing.

O that Thou shouldst give dust a tongue
      To crie to Thee,
And then not hear it crying! All day long
      My heart was in my knee,
         But no hearing.

Therefore my soul lay out of sight,
      Untun'd, unstrung;
My feeble spirit, unable to look right,
      Like a nipt blossome, hung
         Discontented.

O, cheer and tune my heartlesse breast,
      Deferre no time;
That so Thy favours granting my request,
      They and my minde may chime,
         And mend my ryme.

Christmas

All after pleasures as I rid one day,
　My horse and I, both tir'd, bodie and minde,
With full crie of affections, quite astray,
　I took up in the next inne I could finde.

There when I came, whom found I but my deare,
　My dearest Lord, expecting till the grief
Of pleasures brought me to Him, readie there
　To be all passengers' most sweet relief.

O Thou, Whose glorious yet contracted light,
　Wrapt in Night's mantle, stole into a manger,
Since my dark soul and brutish, is Thy right,
　To man, of all beasts, be not Thou a stranger:

Furnish and deck my soul, that Thou mayst have
A better lodging than a rack or grave.

*

The shepherds sing; and shall I silent be?
　My God, no hymne for Thee?
My soul's a shepherd too; a flock it feeds
　Of thoughts and words and deeds:
The pasture is Thy Word; the streams Thy grace,
　Enriching all the place.

Shepherd and flock shall sing, and all my powers
　Out-sing the daylight houres;
Then we will chide the Sunne for letting Night
　Take up his place and right:
We sing one common Lord; wherefore he should
　Himself the candle hold.

I will go searching till I finde a sunne
　Shall stay till we have done;
A willing shiner, that shall shine as gladly
　As frost-nipt sunnes look sadly:
Then we will sing, and shine all our own day,
　And one another pay:

His beams shall cheer my breast, and both so twine,
Till ev'n His beams sing, and my music shine.

Ungratefulnesse

Lord, with what bountie and rare clemencie
    Hast Thou redeem'd us from the grave!
        If Thou hadst let us runne,
    Gladly had man ador'd the sunne,
        And thought his god most brave,
Where now we shall be better gods then he.

Thou hast but two rare cabinets full of treasure,
    The Trinitie and Incarnation;
        Thou hast unlockt them both,
    And made them jewels to betroth
        The work of Thy creation
Unto Thyself in everlasting pleasure.

The statelier cabinet is the Trinitie,
    Whose sparkling light access denies:
        Therefore thou dost not show
    This fully to us till death blow
        The dust into our eyes;
For by that powder Thou wilt make us see.

But all Thy sweets are packt up in the other;
    Thy mercies thither flock and flow,
        That as the first affrights,
    This may allure us with delights;
        Because this box we know,
For we have all of us just such another.

But man is close, reserv'd, and dark to Thee;
    When Thou demandest but a heart,
        He cavils instantly:
    In his poore cabinet of bone
        Sinnes have their box apart,
Defrauding Thee, Who gavest two for one.

Sighs and Grones

O do not use me
After my sinnes! look not on my desert,
But on Thy glorie; then Thou wilt reform,
And not refuse me; for Thou onely art
The mightie God, but I a sillie worm:
      O, do not bruise me!

O, do not urge me;
For what account can Thy ill steward make?
I have abus'd Thy flock, destroy'd Thy woods,
Suckt all Thy magazens; my head did ake,
Till it found out how to consume Thy goods:
      O, do not scourge me!

O, do not blinde me!
I have deserv'd that an Egyptian night
Should thicken all my powers, because my lust
Hath still sow'd fig-leaves to exclude Thy light;
But I am frailtie, and already dust:
      O, do not grinde me!

O, do not fill me
With the turn'd viall of Thy bitter wrath
For Thou hast other vessels full of blood,
A part whereof my Saviour empti'd hath,
Ev'n unto death: since He died for my good,
      O, do not kill me!

But O, reprieve me!
For Thou hast life and death at Thy command;
Thou art both Judge and Saviour, feast and rod,
Cordiall and corrosive: put not Thy hand
Into the bitter box; but, O my God,
      My God, relieve me!

The World

Love built a stately house, where Fortune came;
And spinning phansies, she was heard to say
That her fine cobwebs did support the frame,
Whereas they were supported by the same;
But Wisdome quickly swept them all away.

Then Pleasure came, who, liking not the fashion,
Began to make balcónes, terraces,
Till she had weaken'd all by alteration;
But rev'rend laws, and many a proclamation,
Reformèd all at length with menaces.

Then enter'd Sinne, and with that sycomore
Whose leaves first sheltred man from drought and dew,
Working and winding slily evermore,
The inward walls and sommers cleft and tore;
But Grace shor'd these, and cut that as it grew.

Then Sinne combin'd with Death in a firm band
To rase the building to the very floore:
Which they effected, none could them withstand;
But Love and Grace took Glorie by the hand,
And built a braver palace then before.

Our Life Is Hid with Christ in God

Colossians III: 3

My words and thoughts do both expresse this notion,
That LIFE hath with the sun a double motion.
The first Is straight, and our diurnall friend;
The other HID, and doth obliquely bend.
One life is wrapt IN flesh, and tends to earth;
The other winds towards HIM, Whose happie birth
Taught me to live here so THAT still one eye
Should aim and shoot at that which Is on high;
 Quitting with daily labour all MY pleasure,
  To gain at harvest an eternall TREASURE.

Vanitie

The fleet astronomer can bore
And thred the spheres with his quick-piercing minde;
He views their stations, walks from doore to doore,
    Surveys as if he had design'd
To make a purchase there; he sees their dances,
    And knoweth long before
Both their full-ey'd aspécts and secret glances.

The nimble diver with his side
Cuts through the working waves, that he may fetch
His dearly-earnèd pearl; which God did hide
    On purpose from the venturous wretch,
That He might save his life, and also hers
    Who with excessive pride
Her own destruction and his danger wears.

The subtil chymick can devest
And strip the creature naked, till he finde
The callow principles within their nest:
    There he imparts to them his minde,
Admitted to their bed-chamber before
    They appeare trim and drest
To ordinarie suitours at the doore.

What hath not man sought out and found,
But his deare God? Who yet His glorious law
Embosomes in us, mellowing the ground
    With showers and frosts, with love and aw,
So that we need not say, Where's this command?
    Poore man, thou searchest round
To find out death, but missest life at hand!

Lent

Welcome, deare feast of Lent! who loves not thee,
He loves not temperance or authoritie,
  But is compos'd of passion.
The Scriptures bid us fast: the Church says, 'Now
Give to thy Mother what thou wouldst allow
  To ev'ry corporation.'

The humble soul, compos'd of love and fear,
Begins at home, and layes the burden there,
  When doctrines disagree;
He sayes, 'In things which use hath justly got
I am a scandall to the Church, and not
  The Church is so to me.'

True Christians should be glad of an occasion
To use their temperance, seeking no evasion,
  When good is seasonable;
Unlesse authoritie, which should increase
The obligation in us, make it lesse,
  And power it self disable.

Besides the cleannesse of sweet abstinence,
Quick thoughts, and motions at a small expense,
  A face not fearing light;
Whereas in fulnesse there are sluttish fumes,
Sowre exhalations, and dishonest rheumes,
  Revenging the delight.

Then those same pendant profits, which the Spring
And Easter intimate, enlarge the thing
  And goodnesse of the deed;
Neither ought other men's abuse of Lent
Spoil the good use, lest by that argument
  We forfeit all our creed.

It's true we cannot reach Christ's forti'th day
Yet to go part of that religious way
  Is better then to rest:
We cannot reach our Saviour's puritie;
Yet are we bid, 'Be holy ev'n as He':
  In both let's do our best.

Who goeth in the way which Christ hath gone
Is much more sure to meet with Him then one
　　　That travelleth by-wayes;
Perhaps my God, though He be farre before,
May turn, and take me by the hand, and more,
　　　May strengthen my decayes.

Yet, Lord, instruct us to improve our fast
By starving sinne, and taking such repast
　　　As may our faults controll;
That ev'ry man may revell at his doore,
Not in his parlour – banquetting the poore,
　　　And among those, his soul.

Vertue

Sweet day, so cool, so calm, so bright,
The bridall of the earth and skie,
The dew shall weep thy fall to-night;
　　　For thou must die.

Sweet rose, whose hue angrie and brave
Bids the rash gazer wipe his eye,
Thy root is ever in its grave,
　　　And thou must die.

Sweet spring, full of sweet days and roses,
A box where sweets compacted lie,
My musick shows ye have your closes,
　　　And all must die.

Onely a sweet and vertuous soul,
Like season'd timber, never gives;
But though the whole world turn to coal,
　　　Then chiefly lives.

The Pearl

Matthew XIII

I know the wayes of Learning; both the head
And pipes that feed the presse, and make it runne;
What Reason hath from Nature borrowèd,
Or of itself, like a good huswife, spunne
In laws and policie; what the starres conspire,
What willing Nature speaks, what forc'd by fire;
Both th' old discoveries and the new-found seas,
The stock and surplus, cause and historie, –
All these stand open, or I have the keyes:
           Yet I love Thee.

I know the wayes of Honour, what maintains
The quick returns of courtesie and wit;
In vies of favours whether partie gains;
When glorie swells the heart, and moldeth it
To all expressions both of hand and eye;
Which on the world a true-love knot may tie,
And bear the bundle, wheresoe're it goes;
How many drammes of spirit there must be
To sell my life unto my friends or foes:
           Yet I love Thee.

I know the wayes of pleasure, the sweet strains,
The lullings and the relishes of it;
The propositions of hot bloud and brains;
What mirth and musick mean; what Love and Wit
Have done these twentie hundred years and more;
I know the projects of unbridled store:
My stuffe is flesh, not brasse; my senses live,
And grumble oft that they have more in me
Then He that curbs them, being but one to five:
           Yet I love Thee.

I know all these, and have them in my hand:
Therefore not seelèd, but with open eyes
I flie to Thee, and fully understand
Both the main sale and the commodities;

And at what rate and price I have Thy love,
With all the circumstances that may move:
Yet through the labyrinths, not my groveling wit,
But Thy silk-twist let down from heav'n to me,
Did both conduct and teach me how by it
        To climb to Thee.

Affliction

Broken in pieces all asunder,
    Lord, hunt me not,
    A thing forgot,
Once a poor creature, now a wonder,
  A wonder tortur'd in the space
  Betwixt this world and that of grace.

My thoughts are all a case of knives,
    Wounding my heart
    With scatter'd smart,
As wat'ring-pots give flowers their lives;
  Nothing their furie can controll
  While they do wound and prick my soul.

All my attendants are at strife,
    Quitting their place
    Unto my face;
Nothing performs the task of life:
  The elements are let loose to fight,
  And while I live trie out their right.

Oh help, my God! let not their plot
    Kill them and me,
    And also Thee,
Who art my life; dissolve the knot,
  As the sunne scatters by his light
  All the rebellions of the night.

Then shall those powers which work for grief
    Enter Thy pay,
    And day by day
Labour Thy praise and my relief;
  With care and courage building me
  Till I reach heav'n, and, much more, Thee.

Man

    My God, I heard this day
That none doth build a stately habitation
  But he that means to dwell therein.
  What house more stately hath there been,
Or can be, then is Man? to whose creation
    All things are in decay.

    For Man is ev'ry thing,
And more: he is a tree, yet bears mo fruit;
  A beast, yet is, or should be, more:
  Reason and speech we onely bring;
Parrats may thank us, if they are not mute,
    They go upon the score.

    Man is all symmetrie,
Full of proportions, one limbe to another,
  And all to all the world besides;
  Each part may call the farthest brother,
For head with foot hath private amitie,
    And both with moons and tides.

    Nothing hath got so farre
But Man hath caught and kept it as his prey;
  His eyes dismount the highest starre;
  He is in little all the sphere;
Herbs gladly cure our flesh, because that they
    Finde their acquaintance there.

For us the windes do blow,
The earth doth rest, heav'n move, and fountains flow;
    Nothing we see but means our good,
    As our delight or as our treasure;
The whole is either our cupboard of food
        Or cabinet of pleasure.

    The starres have us to bed,
Night draws the curtain, which the sunne withdraws;
    Musick and light attend our head,
    All things unto our flesh are kinde
In their descent and being; to our minde
        In their ascent and cause.

    Each thing is full of dutie:
Waters united are our navigation;
    Distinguishèd, our habitation;
    Below, our drink; above, our meat;
Both are our cleanlinesse. Hath one such beautie?
        Then how are all things neat!

    More servants wait on Man
Than he'l take notice of: in ev'ry path
    He treads down that which doth befriend him
    When sicknesse makes him pale and wan.
Oh mightie love! Man is one world, and hath
        Another to attend him.

    Since then, my God, Thou hast
So brave a palace built, O dwell in it,
    That it may dwell with Thee at last!
    Till then afford us so much wit,
That, as the world serves us, we may serve Thee,
        And both Thy servants be.

Antiphon

Chor. Praisèd be the God of love
  Men. Here below,
  Ang. And here above;
Chor. Who hath dealt his mercies so
  Ang. To His friend,
  Men. And to His foe;

Chor. That both grace and glorie tend
  Ang. Us of old,
  Men. And us in th' end
Chor. The great Shepherd of the fold
  Ang. Us did make,
  Men. For us was sold.

Chor. He our foes in pieces brake:
  Ang. Him we touch,
  Men. And Him we take.
Chor. Wherefore, since that He is such,
  Ang. We adore,
  Men. And we do crouch.

Chor. Lord, Thy praises should bee more.
  Men. We have none,
  Ang. And we no store;
Chor. Praisèd be the God alone
  Who hath made of two folds one.

Unkindnesse

Lord, make me coy and tender to offend:
In friendship, first I think if that agree
      Which I intend
    Unto my friend's intent and end;
I would not use a friend as I use Thee.

If any touch my friend or his good name,
It is my honour and my love to free
      His blasted fame
    From the least spot or thought of blame:
I could not use a friend as I use Thee.

My friend may spit upon my curious floore
Would he have gold? I lend it instantly;
      But let the poore,
    And Thou within them, starve at doore:
I cannot use a friend as I use Thee.

When that my friend pretendeth to a place,
I quit my interest, and leave it free;
      But when Thy grace
    Sues for my heart, I Thee displace;
Nor would I use a friend as I use Thee.

Yet can a friend what Thou hast done fulfill?
O, write in brass, 'My God upon a tree
      His bloud did spill,
    Onely to purchase my good-will:'
Yet use I not my foes as I use Thee.

Life

I made a posie while the day ran by:
Here will I smell my remnant out, and tie
    My life within this band;
But Time did becken to the flow'rs, and they
By noon most cunningly did steal away,
    And wither'd in my hand.

My hand was next to them, and then my heart;
I took, without more thinking, in good part
    Time's gentle admonition;
Who did so sweetly Death's sad taste convey,
Making my minde to smell my fatall day,
    Yet sugring the suspicion.

Farewell, deare flow'rs; sweetly your time ye spent,
Fit while ye lived for smell or ornament,
    And after death for cures.
I follow straight, without complaints or grief;
Since if my scent be good, I care not if
    It be as short as yours.

Submission

But that Thou art my wisdome, Lord,
    And both mine eyes are Thine,
My minde would be extreamly stirr'd
    For missing my designe.

Were it not better to bestow
    Some place and power on me?
Then should Thy praises with me grow,
    And share in my degree.

But when I thus dispute and grieve,
    I do resume my fight;
And pilfring what I once did give,
    Disseize Thee of Thy right.

How know I, if Thou shouldst me raise,
    That I should then raise Thee?
Perhaps great places and Thy praise
    Do not so well agree.

Wherefore unto my gift I stand,
    I will no more advise;
Onely do Thou lend me a hand,
    Since Thou hast both mine eyes.

Justice

I cannot skill of these Thy wayes
Lord, Thou didst make me, yet Thou woundest me;
Lord, Thou dost wound me, yet Thou dost relieve me;
Lord, Thou relievest, yet I die by Thee;
Lord, Thou dost kill me, yet Thou dost reprieve me.

But when I mark my life and praise,
    Thy justice me most fitly payes;
For I do praise Thee, yet I praise Thee not;
My prayers mean Thee, yet my prayers stray;
I would do well, yet sinne the hand hath got;
My soul doth love Thee, yet it loves delay;
    I cannot skill of these my ways.

Charms and Knots

Who reade a chapter when they rise,
Shall ne're be troubled with ill eyes.

A poor man's rod, when Thou dost ride,
Is both a weapon and a guide.

Who shuts his hand hath lost his gold;
Who opens it hath it twice-told.

Who goes to bed and doth not pray
Maketh two nights to ev'ry day.

Who by aspersions throw a stone
At th' head of others, hit their own.

Who looks on ground with humble eyes
Findes himself there, and seeks to rise.

When th' hair is sweet through pride or lust,
The powder doth forget the dust.

Take one from ten, and what remains?
Ten still, if sermons go for gains.

In shallow waters heav'n doth show;
But who drinks on, to hell may go.

Affliction

My God, I read this day
That planted Paradise was not so firm
As was and is Thy floting Ark, whose stay
And anchor Thou art onely, to confirm
And strengthen it in ev'ry age,
When waves do rise and tempests rage.

At first we liv'd in pleasure,
Thine own delights Thou didst to us impart;
When we grew wanton, Thou didst use displeasure
To make us Thine; yet that we might not part,
As we at first did board with Thee,
Now Thou wouldst taste our miserie.

There is but joy and grief:
If either will convert us, we are Thine;
Some angels us'd the first; if our relief
Take up the second, then Thy double line
And sev'rall baits in either kinde
Furnish Thy table to Thy minde.

Affliction, then, is ours;
We are the trees, whom shaking fastens more;
While blustring windes destroy the wanton bowres,
And ruffle all their curious knots and store.
My God, so temper joy and wo
That Thy bright beams may tame Thy Bow.

Mortification

How soon doth man decay!
When clothes are taken from a chest of sweets
　　To swaddle infants, whose young breath
　　　　Scarce knows the way,
　　Those clouts are little winding-sheets,
Which do consign and send them unto Death.

　　When boyes go first to bed,
They step into their voluntarie graves;
　　Sleep binds them fast, onely their breath
　　　　Makes them not dead:
　　Successive nights, like rolling waves,
Convey them quickly who are bound for Death.

　　When Youth is frank and free,
And calls for musick, while his veins do swell,
　　All day exchanging mirth and breath
　　　　In companie,
　　That musick summons to the knell
Which shall befriend him at the house of Death.

　　When man grows staid and wise,
Getting a house and home, where he may move
　　Within the circle of his breath,
　　　　Schooling his eyes,
　　That dumbe inclosure maketh love
Unto the coffin that attends his death.

　　When Age grows low and weak,
Marking his grave, and thawing ev'ry year,
　　Till all do melt and drown his breath
　　　　When he would speak,
　　A chair or litter shows the biere
Which shall convey him to the house of Death.

　　Man, ere he is aware,
Hath put together a solemnitie,
　　And drest his hearse, while he has breath
　　　　As yet to spare;
　　Yet, Lord, instruct us so to die,
That all these dyings may be LIFE in DEATH.

Decay

Sweet were the days when Thou didst lodge with Lot,
Struggle with Jacob, sit with Gideon,
Advise with Abraham; when Thy power could not
Encounter Moses' strong complaints and mone:
  Thy words were then, 'Let Me alone.'

One might have sought and found Thee presently
At some fair oak, or bush, or cave, or well:
'Is my God this way?' 'No,' they would reply;
'He is to Sinai gone, as we heard tell;
  List, ye may heare great Aaron's bell.'

But now Thou dost Thyself immure and close
In some one corner of a feeble heart;
Where yet both Sinne and Satan, Thy old foes,
Do pinch and straiten Thee, and use much art
  To gain Thy thirds and little part.

I see the world grows old, when, as the heat
Of Thy great love, – once spread, – as in an urn
Doth closet up itself, and still retreat,
Cold Sinne still forcing it, – till it return,
  And calling Justice, all things burn.

Miserie

Lord, Let the angels praise Thy name:
Man is a foolish thing, a foolish thing;
 Folly and sinne play all his game;
His house still burns, and yet he still doth sing –
   'Man is but grasse,
  He knows it – Fill the glasse.'

How canst Thou brook his foolishnesse?
Why, he'l not lose a cup of drink for Thee:
 Bid him but temper his excesse,
Not he: he knows where he can better be –
   As he will swear –
  Then to serve Thee in fear.

What strange pollutions doth he wed,
And make his own! as if none knew but he.
   No man shall beat into his head
That Thou within his curtains drawn canst see:
      They are of cloth,
      Where never yet came moth.

   The best of men, turn but Thy hand
For one poore minute, stumble at a pinne;
   They would not have their actions scann'd,
Nor any sorrow tell them that they sinne,
      Though it be small,
      And measure not their fall.

   They quarrell Thee, and would give over
The bargain made to serve Thee; but Thy love
   Holds them unto it, and doth cover
Their follies with the wing of Thy milde Dove,
      Not suff'ring those
      Who would, to be Thy foes.

   My God, man cannot praise Thy name:
Thou art all brightnesse, perfect puritie;
   The sunne holds down his head for shame,
Dead with eclipses, when we speak of Thee:
      How shall infection
      Presume on Thy perfection?

   As dirtie hands foule all they touch,
And those things most which are most pure and fine,
   So our clay-hearts, ev'n when we crouch
To sing Thy praises, make them less divine:
      Yet either this
      Or none Thy portion is.

   Man cannot serve Thee: let him go
And serve the swine – there, there is his delight:
   He doth not like this vertue, no;
Give him his dirt to wallow in all night:
      'These preachers make
      His head to shoot and ake.'

O foolish man! where are thine eyes?
How hast thou lost them in a crowd of cares!
   Thou pull'st the rug, and wilt not rise,
No, not to purchase the whole pack of starres:
      'There let them shine;
      Thou must go sleep, or dine.'

The bird that sees a daintie bowre
Made in the tree, where she was wont to sit,
   Wonders and sings, but not His power
Who made the arbor; this exceeds her wit.
      But Man doth know
      The spring whence all things flow:

And yet, as though he knew it not,
His knowledge winks, and lets his humours reigne;
   They make his life a constant blot,
And all the bloud of God to run in vain.
      Ah, wretch! what verse
      Can thy strange wayes rehearse?

Indeed, at first Man was a treasure,
A box of jewels, shop of rarities,
   A ring whose posie was 'My pleasure';
He was a garden in a Paradise;
      Glorie and grace
      Did crown his heart and face.

But sinne hath fool'd him; now he is
A lump of flesh, without a foot or wing
   To raise him to the glimpse of blisse;
A sick-toss'd vessel, dashing on each thing,
      Nay his own shelf:
      My God, I mean myself.

Jordan

When first my lines of heav'nly joyes made mention,
Such was their lustre, they did so excell,
That I sought out quaint words and trim invention;
My thoughts began to burnish, sprout, and swell,
Curling with metaphors a plain intention,
Decking the sense as if it were to sell.

Thousands of notions in my brain did runne,
Off'ring their service, if I were not sped:
I often blotted what I had begunne –
This was not quick enough, and that was dead;
Nothing could seem too rich to clothe the sunne,
Much lesse those joyes which trample on his head.

As flames do work and winde when they ascend,
So did I weave myselfe into the sense;
But while I bustled I might hear a friend
Whisper, 'How wide is all this long pretence!
There is in love a sweetnesse ready penn'd;
Copie out onely that, and save expense.'

Prayer

Of what an easie quick accesse,
My blessèd Lord, art Thou! how suddenly
    May our requests Thine ears invade!
To show that State dislikes not easinesse,
If I but lift mine eyes my suit is made;
Thou canst no more not heare then Thou canst die.

Of what supreme almightie power
Is Thy great arm, which spans the east and west
    And tacks the centre to the sphere!
By it do all things live their measur'd houre;
We cannot ask the thing which is not there,
Blaming the shallownesse of our request.

Of what unmeasurable love
Art Thou possest, Who, when Thou could'st not die,
   Wert fain to take our flesh and curse,
And for our sakes in person sinne reprove;
That by destroying that which ty'd Thy purse,
Thou mightst make way for liberalitie!

Since, then, these three wait on Thy throne,
Ease, Power, and Love, I value Prayer so,
   That were I to leave all but one,
Wealth, fame, endowments, vertues, all should go;
I and deare Prayer would together dwell,
And quickly gain for each inch lost an ell.

Obedience

   My God, if writings may
   Convey a lordship any way
Whither the buyer and the seller please,
   Let it not Thee displease
If this poore paper do as much as they.

   On it my heart doth bleed
   As many lines as there doth need
To passe itself and all it hath to Thee;
   To which I do agree,
And here present it as my speciall deed.

   If that hereafter Pleasure
   Cavill, and claim her part and measure,
As if this passèd with a reservation,
   Or some such words in fashion,
I here exclude the wrangler from Thy treasure.

   O, let Thy sacred will
   All Thy delight in me fulfill!
Let me not think an action mine own way,
   But as Thy love shall sway,
Resigning up the rudder to Thy skill.

Lord, what is man to Thee,
That Thou shouldst minde a rotten tree!
Yet since Thou canst not choose but see my actions,
So great are Thy perfections,
Thou mayst as well my actions guide as see.

Besides, Thy death and bloud
Show'd a strange love to all our good;
Thy sorrows were in earnest, no faint proffer,
Or superficial offer
Of what we might not take or be withstood.

Wherefore I all forego:
To one word onely I say, No;
Where in the deed there was an intimation
Of a gift or donation,
Lord, let it now by way of purchase go.

He that will passe his land,
As I have mine, may set his hand
And heart unto this deed, when he hath read,
And make the purchase spread
To both our goods, if he to it will stand.

How happie were my part,
If some kinde man would thrust his heart
Into these lines, till in heav'n's Court of Rolls
They were by wingèd souls
Entred for both, farre above their desert!

Conscience

Peace, pratler, do not lowre:
Not a fair look but thou dost call it foul,
Not a sweet dish but thou dost call it sowre;
 Musick to thee doth howl.
 By list'ning to thy chatting fears
 I have both lost mine eyes and eares.

 Pratler, no more, I say;
My thoughts must work, but like a noiselesse sphere
Harmonious peace must rock them all the day:
 No room for pratlers there.
 If thou persistest, I will tell thee
 That I have physick to expell thee.

 And the receit shall be
My Saviour's bloud: whenever at His board
I do but taste it, straight it cleanseth me,
 And leaves thee not a word;
 No, not a tooth or nail to scratch,
 And at my actions carp or catch.

 Yet if thou talkest still,
Besides my physick know there's some for thee;
Some wood and nails to make a staffe or bill
 For those that trouble me:
 The bloudie crosse of my deare Lord
 Is both my physick and my sword.

Sion

Lord, with what glorie wast Thou serv'd of old,
When Solomon's temple stood and flourishèd!
　　Where most things were of purest gold;
　　The wood was all embellishèd
With flowers and carvings mysticall and rare;
All show'd the builders crav'd the seer's care.

Yet all this glorie, all this pomp and state,
Did not affect Thee much, was not Thy aim:
　　Something there was that sow'd debate;
　　Wherefore Thou quit'st Thy ancient claim,
And now Thy architecture meets with sinne,
For all Thy frame and fabrick is within.

There Thou art struggling with a peevish heart,
Which sometimes crosseth Thee, Thou sometimes it;
　　The fight is hard on either part:
　　Great God doth fight, He doth submit.
All Solomon's sea of brasse and world of stone
Is not so deare to Thee as one good grone.

And truly brasse and stones are heavie things –
Tombes for the dead, not temples fit for Thee;
　　But grones are quick, and full of wings,
　　And all their motions upward be;
And ever as they mount like larks they sing;
The note is sad, yet musick for a king.

Home

Come, Lord, my head doth burn, my heart is sick,
   While Thou dost ever, ever stay;
Thy long deferrings wound me to the quick,
   My spirit gaspeth night and day:
      O, show Thyself to me,
      Or take me up to Thee!

How canst Thou stay, considering the pace
   The bloud did make which Thou didst waste?
When I behold it trickling down Thy face,
   I never saw thing make such haste:
      O, show Thyself to me,
      Or take me up to Thee!

When man was lost, Thy pitie lookt about
   To see what help in th' earth or skie;
But there was none, at least no help without;
   The help did in Thy bosom lie:
      O, show Thyself to me,
      Or take me up to Thee!

There lay Thy Sonne; and must He leave that nest,
   That hive of sweetnesse, to remove
Thraldom from those who would not at a feast
   Leave one poore apple for Thy love?
      O, show Thyself to me,
      Or take me up to Thee!

He did, He came: O, my Redeemer deare,
   After all this canst Thou be strange?
So many yeares baptiz'd, and not appeare,
   As if Thy love could fail or change?
      O, show Thyself to me,
      Or take me up to Thee!

Yet if Thou stayest still, why must I stay?
  My God, what is this world to me?
This world of wo. Hence, all ye clouds; away,
    Away; I must get up and see:
      O, show Thyself to me,
      Or take me up to Thee!

What is this weary world, this meat and drink,
  That chains us by the teeth so fast?
What is this woman-kinde, which I can wink
    Into a blacknesse and distaste?
      O, show Thyself to me,
      Or take me up to Thee!

With one small sigh Thou gav'st me th' other day
  I blasted all the joyes about me,
And scouling on them as they pin'd away,
    'Now come again,' said I, 'and flout me.'
      O, show Thyself to me,
      Or take me up to Thee!

Nothing but drought and dearth, but bush and brake,
  Which way so-e're I look, I see;
Some may dream merrily, but when they wake,
    They dresse themselves and come to Thee:
      O, show Thyself to me,
      Or take me up to Thee!

We talk of harvests – there are no such things
  But when we leave our corn and hay;
There is no fruitful yeare but that which brings
    The last and lov'd, though dreadfull day:
      O, show Thyself to me,
      Or take me up to Thee!

Oh, loose this frame, this knot of man untie;
  That my free soul may use her wing,
Which now is pinion'd with mortalitie,
    As an intangl'd, hamper'd thing:
      O, show Thyself to me,
      Or take me up to Thee!

What have I left, that I should stay and grone?
    The most of me to heav'n is fled;
My thoughts and joyes are all packt up and gone,
    And for their old acquaintance plead:
        O, show Thyself to me,
        Or take me up to Thee!

Come, dearest Lord, passe not this holy season,
    My flesh and bones and joynts do pray;
And ev'n my verse, when by the ryme and reason
    The word is 'Stay,' says ever, 'Come':
        O, show Thyself to me,
        Or take me up to Thee!

The British Church

I joy, deare Mother, when I view
Thy perfect lineaments, and hue
        Both sweet and bright.

Beauty in thee takes up her place,
And dates her letters from thy face,
        When she doth write.

A fine aspéct in fit aray,
Neither too mean nor yet too gay,
        Shows who is best.

Outlandish looks may not compare;
For all they either painted are,
        Or else undrest.

She on the hills, which wantonly
Allureth all in hope to be
        By her preferr'd,

Hath kiss'd so long her painted shrines,
That ev'n her face by kissing shines,
        For her reward.

She in the valley is so shie
Of dressing, that her hair doth lie
                About her eares;

While she avoids her neighbour's pride,
She wholly goes on th' other side,
                And nothing wears.

But, dearest Mother, what those misse,
The mean thy praise and glorie is,
                And long may be.

Blessèd be God, Whose love it was
To double-moat thee with His grace,
                And none but thee.

The Quip

The merrie World did on a day
With his train-bands and mates agree
To meet together where I lay,
And all in sport to geere at me.

First Beautie crept into a rose,
Which when I pluckt not, 'Sir,' said she,
'Tell me, I pray, whose hands are those?'
But Thou shalt answer, Lord, for me.

Then Money came, and chinking still,
'What tune is this, poore man?' said he;
'I heard in Musick you had skill':
But Thou shalt answer, Lord, for me.

Then came brave Glorie puffing by
In silks that whistled, who but he!
He scarce allowed me half an eie:
But Thou shalt answer, Lord, for me.

Then came quick Wit and Conversation,
And he would needs a comfort be,
And, to be short, make an oration:
But Thou shalt answer, Lord, for me.

Yet when the houre of Thy designe
To answer these fine things shall come,
Speak not at large, say, I am Thine,
And then they have their answer home.

Vanitie

Poore silly soul, whose hope and head lies low,
Whose flat delights on earth do creep and grow;
To whom the starres shine not so faire as eyes,
Nor solid work as false embroyderies, –
Heark and beware, lest what you now do measure
And write for sweet prove a most sowre displeasure.

O, heare betimes, lest thy relenting
        May come too late;
To purchase heaven for repenting
        Is no hard rate.

If souls be made of earthly mould,
        Let them love gold;
        If born on high,
Let them unto their kindred flie;
For they can never be at rest
Till they regain their ancient nest.

Then, silly soul, take heed; for earthly joy
Is but a bubble, and makes thee a boy.

The Dawning

Awake, sad heart, whom sorrow ever drowns;
   Take up thine eyes, which feed on earth;
Unfold thy forehead, gathered into frowns;
   Thy Saviour comes, and with Him mirth:
         Awake, awake,
And with a thankfull heart His comforts take.
   But thou dost still lament, and pine, and crie,
   And feel His death, but not His victorie.

Arise, sad heart; if thou dost not withstand,
   Christ's resurrection thine may be;
Do not by hanging down break from the hand
   Which, as it riseth, raiseth thee:
         Arise, arise,
And with His buriall-linen drie thine eyes.
   Christ left His grave-clothes, that we might, when grief
   Draws tears or bloud, not want an handkerchief.

Jesu

Jesu is in my heart, His sacred name
Is deeply carvèd there: but th' other week
A great affliction broke the little frame
Ev'n all to pieces; which I went to seek:
And first I found the corner where was J,
After where ES, and next where U was grav'd.
When I had got these parcels, instantly
I sat me down to spell them, and perceiv'd
That to my broken heart he was I ease you,
        And to my whole is JESU.

Businesse

Canst be idle? canst thou play,
Foolish soul, who sinn'd to day?

Rivers run, and springs each one
Know their home, and get them gone:
Hast thou tears, or hast thou none?

If, poore soul, thou hast no tears,
Would thou hadst no faults or fears!
Who hath these, those ill forbears.

Windes still work – it is their plot,
Be the season cold or hot:
Hast thou sighs, or hast thou not?

If thou hast no sighs or grones,
Would thou hadst no flesh and bones!
Lesser pains scape greater ones.

But if yet thou idle be,
Foolish soul, Who died for thee?

Who did leave His Father's throne
To assume thy flesh and bone?
Had He life, or had He none?

If He had not liv'd for thee,
Thou hadst died most wretchedly,
And two deaths had been thy fee.

He so farre thy good did plot,
That His own self He forgot:
Did He die, or did He not?

If He had not died for thee,
Thou hadst liv'd in miserie;
Two lives worse then ten deaths be.

And hath any space of breath
'Twixt his sinnes' and Saviour's death?

He that loseth gold, though drosse,
Tells to all he meets, his crosse,
He that sinnes, hath he no losse?

He that findes a silver vein
Thinks on it, and thinks again
Brings thy Saviour's death no gain?

Who in heart not ever kneels
Neither sinne nor Saviour feels.

Dialogue

Man
Sweetest Saviour, if my soul
　Were but worth the having,
Quickly should I then controll
　Any thought of waving.
But when all my cares and pains
Cannot give the name of gains
To Thy wretch so full of stains,
What delight or hope remains?

Saviour
What, childe, is the ballance thine,
　Thine the poise and measure?
If I say, 'Thou shalt be Mine,'
　Finger not My treasure.
What the gains in having thee
Do amount to, onely He
Who for man was sold can see;
That transferr'd th' accounts to Me.

Man
But as I can see no merit
　Leading to this favour,

So the way to fit me for it
   Is beyond my savour.
As the reason, then, is Thine,
So the way is none of mine,
I disclaim the whole designe;
Sinne disclaims and I resigne.

      Saviour
That is all: – if that I could
   Get without repining –
And My clay, My creature, would
   Follow my resigning;
That as I did freely part
With My glorie and desert,
Left all joyes to feel all smart –

      Man
Ah, no more: Thou break'st my heart

Dulnesse

Why do I languish thus, drooping and dull,
    As if I were all earth?
O, give me quicknesse, that I may with mirth
    Praise Thee brim-full!

The wanton lover in a curious strain
    Can praise his fairest fair,
And with quaint metaphors her curlèd hair
    Curl o're again.

Thou art my lovelinesse, my life, my light,
    Beautie alone to me;
Thy bloudy death, and undeserv'd, makes Thee
    Pure red and white.

When all perfections as but one appeare,
    That, those, Thy form doth shew,
The very dust where Thou dost tread and go
    Makes beauties here.

Where are my lines, then? my approaches, views?
    Where are my window-songs?
Lovers are still pretending, and ev'n wrongs
    Sharpen their Muse.

But I am lost in flesh, whose sugred lyes
    Still mock me and grow bold:
Sure Thou didst put a minde there, if I could
    Finde where it lies.

Lord, cleare Thy gift, that with a constant wit
    I may but look towards Thee:
Look onely; for to love Thee who can be,
    What angel fit?

Love-Joy

As on a window late I cast mine eye,
I saw a vine drop grapes with J and C
Anneal'd on every bunch. One standing by
Ask'd what it meant. I (who am never loth
To spend my judgement) said: 'It seem'd to me
To be the bodie and the letters both
Of Joy and Charitie.' 'Sir, you have not miss'd,'
    The man reply'd; 'it figures Jesus Christ.'

Providence

O sacred Providence, Who from end to end
Strongly and sweetly movest! shall I write,
And not of Thee, through Whom my fingers bend
To hold my quill? shall they not do Thee right?

Of all the creatures both in sea and land,
Onely to man Thou hast made known Thy wayes,
And put the penne alone into his hand,
And made him secretarie of Thy praise.

Beasts fain would sing; birds dittie to their notes;
Trees would be tuning on their native lute
To Thy renown: but all their hands and throats
Are brought to Man, while they are lame and mute.

Man is the world's high-priest: he doth present
The sacrifice for all; while they below
Unto the service mutter an assent,
Such as springs use that fall, and windes that blow.

He that to praise and laud Thee doth refrain,
Doth not refrain unto himself alone,
But robs a thousand who would praise Thee fain,
And doth commit a world of sinne in one.

The beasts say, 'Eat me'; but if beasts must teach
The tongue is yours to eat, but mine to praise:
The trees say, 'Pull me'; but the hand you stretch
Is mine to write, as it is yours to raise.

Wherefore, most sacred Spirit, I here present,
For me and all my fellows, praise to Thee;
And just it is that I should pay the rent,
Because the benefit accrues to me.

We all acknowledge both Thy power and love
To be exact, transcendent, and divine;
Who dost so strongly and so sweetly move,
While all things have their will, yet none but Thine.

For either Thy command or Thy permission
Lay hands on all; they are Thy right and left:
The first puts on with speed and expedition;
The other curbs Sinne's stealing pace and theft.

Nothing escapes them both; all must appeare,
And be dispos'd, and dress'd, and tun'd by Thee,
Who sweetly temper'st all. If we could heare
Thy skill and art, what musick would it be!

Thou art in small things great, not small in any;
Thy even praise can neither rise nor fall;
Thou art in all things one, in each thing many;
For Thou art infinite in one and all.

Tempests are calm to Thee; they know Thy hand,
And hold it fast, as children do their father's,
Which crie and follow: Thou hast made poore sand
Check the proud sea, ev'n when it swells and gathers.

Thy cupboard serves the world: the meat is set
Where all may reach; no beast but knows his feed:
Birds teach us hawking; fishes have their net;
The great prey on the lesse, they on some weed.

Nothing ingender'd doth prevent his meat;
Flies have their table spread ere they appeare;
Some creatures have in winter what to eat;
Others do sleep, and envie not their cheer.

How finely dost Thou times and seasons spin,
And make a twist checker'd with night and day,
Which, as it lengthens, windes and windes us in,
As bouls go on, but turning all the way!

Each creature hath a wisdome for his good:
The pigeons feed their tender offspring, crying
When they are callow, but withdraw their food
When they are fledged, that need may teach them flying.

Bees work for man; and yet they never bruise
Their master's flow'r, but leave it, having done,
As fair as ever and as fit to use;
So both the flow'r doth stay and hony run.

Sheep eat the grasse, and dung the ground for more;
Trees after bearing drop their leaves for soil;
Springs vent their streams, and by expense get store;
Clouds cool by heat, and baths by cooling boil.

Who hath the vertue to express the rare
And curious vertues both of herbs and stones?
Is there an herb for that? O that Thy care
Would show a root that gives expressions!

And if an herb hath power, what hath the starres?
A rose, besides his beautie, is a cure:
Doubtlesse our plagues and plentie, peace and warres,
Are there much surer then our art is sure.

Thou hast hid metals: man may take them thence,
But at his perill; when he digs the place
He makes a grave; as if the thing had sense,
And threaten'd man that he should fill the space.

Ev'n poysons praise Thee: should a thing be lost?
Should creatures want, for want of heed, their due?
Since where are poysons antidots are most;
The help stands close, and keeps the fear in view.

The sea, which seems to stop the traveller,
Is by a ship the speedier passage made;
The windes, who think they rule the mariner,
Are rul'd by him, and taught to serve his trade.

And as Thy house is full, so I adore
Thy curious art in marshalling Thy goods.
The hills with health abound, the vales with store;
The South with marble; North with furres and woods.

Hard things are glorious, easie things good cheap;
The common all men have; that which is rare
Men therefore seek to have, and care to keep.
The healthy frosts with Summer-fruits compare.

Light without winde is glasse; warm without weight
Is wooll and furres; cool without closenesse, shade;
Speed without pains, a horse; tall without height,
A servile hawk; low without losse, a spade.

All countries have enough to serve their need:
If they seek fine things, Thou dost make them run
For their offence, and then dost turn their speed
To be commerce and trade from sunne to sunne.

Nothing wears clothes but man; nothing doth need
But he to wear them; nothing useth fire
But man alone, to show his heav'nly breed;
And onely he hath fuel in desire.

When th' earth was dry, Thou mad'st a sea of wet;
When that lay gather'd, Thou didst broach the mountains;
When yet some places could no moisture get,
The windes grew gard'ners, and the clouds good fountains.

Rain, do not hurt my flowers, but gently spend
Your honey-drops: presse not to smell them here;
When they are ripe, their odour will ascend,
And at your lodging with their thanks appeare.

How harsh are thorns to pears! and yet they make
A better hedge, and need lesse reparation.
How smooth are silks comparèd with a stake
Or with a stone! yet make no good foundation.

Sometimes Thou dost divide Thy gifts to man,
Sometimes unite; the Indian nut alone
Is clothing, meat and trencher, drink and can,
Boat, cable, sail, and needle, all in one.

Most herbs that grow in brooks are hot and dry,
Cold fruits' warm kernells help against the winde;
The lemmon's juice and rinde cure mutually;
The whey of milk doth loose, the milk doth binde.

Thy creatures leap not, but expresse a feast,
Where all the guests sit close, and nothing wants:
Frogs marry fish and flesh; bats, bird and beast;
Sponges, non-sense and sense; mines, th' earth and plants.

To show Thou art not bound, as if Thy lot
Were worse then ours, sometimes Thou shiftest hands:
Most things move th' under-jaw, the crocodile not;
Most things sleep lying, th' elephant leans or stands.

But who hath praise enough? nay, who hath any;
None can expresse Thy works but he that knows them;
And none can know Thy works, which are so many
And so complete, but onely He that owes them.

All things that are, though they have sev'rall wayes,
Yet in their being joyn with one advise
To honour Thee; and so I give thee praise
In all my other hymnes, but in this twice.

Each thing that is, although in use and name
It go for one, hath many wayes in store
To honour Thee; and so each hymne Thy fame
Extolleth many wayes, yet this one more.

Hope

I gave to Hope a watch of mine; but he
    An anchor gave to me.
Then an old Prayer-book I did present;
    And he an optick sent.
With that I gave a vial full of tears;
    But he, a few green eares.
Ah, loyterer! I'le no more, no more I'le bring:
    I did expect a ring.

Sinne's Round

Sorrie I am, my God, sorrie I am
That my offences course it in a ring.
My thoughts are working like a busie flame,
Until their cockatrice they hatch and bring:
And when they once have perfected their draughts,
My words take fire from my inflamèd thoughts.

My words take fire from my inflamèd thoughts,
Which spit it forth like the Sicilian hill;
They vent the wares, and passe them with their faults,
And by their breathing ventilate the ill;
But words suffice not; where are lewd intentions,
My hands do joyn to finish the inventions.

My hands do joyn to finish the inventions,
And so my sinnes ascend three stories high,
As Babel grew before there were dissentions.
Yet ill deeds loyter not; for they supplie
New thoughts of sinning: wherefore, to my shame,
Sorrie I am, my God, sorrie I am.

Time

Meeting with Time, 'Slack thing,' said I,
'Thy sithe is dull; whet it, for shame.'
'No marvell, sir,' he did replie,
'If it at length deserve some blame;
    But where one man would have me grind it,
    Twentie for one too sharp do finde it.'

'Perhaps some such of old did passe,
Who above all things lov'd this life;
To whom thy sithe a hatchet was,
Which now is but a pruning-knife.
    Christ's coming hath made man thy debtor,
    Since by thy cutting he grows better.

'And in his blessing thou art blest;
For where thou onely wert before
An executioner at best,
Thou art a gard'ner now; and more,
    An usher to convey our souls
    Beyond the utmost starres and poles.

'And this is that makes life so long,
While it detains us from our God;
Ev'n pleasures here increase the wrong,
And length of dayes lengthens the rod.
    Who wants the place where God doth dwell,
    Partakes already half of hell.

'Of what strange length must that needs be
Which ev'n eternitie excludes!'
Thus farre Time heard me patiently;
Then chafing said: 'This man deludes;
    What do I here before his doore?
    He doth not crave lesse time, but more.'

Gratefulnesse

Thou that hast giv'n so much to me,
Give one thing more, a gratefull heart:
See how Thy beggar works on Thee
    By art:

He makes thy gifts occasion more,
And sayes, If he in this be crost,
All Thou hast given him heretofore
    Is lost.

But Thou didst reckon, when at first
Thy word our hearts and hands did crave,
What it would come to at the worst
    To save.

Perpetuall knockings at Thy doore,
Tears sullying Thy transparent rooms,
Gift upon gift; much would have more,
    And comes.

This notwithstanding, Thou went'st on,
And didst allow us all our noise;
Nay, Thou hast made a sigh and grone
    Thy joyes.

Not that Thou hast not still above
Much better tunes then grones can make,
But that these countrey-aires Thy love
    Did take.

Wherefore I crie, and crie again,
And in no quiet canst Thou be,
Till I a thankfull heart obtain
    Of Thee.

Not thankfull when it pleaseth me,
As if Thy blessings had spare dayes;
But such a heart whose pulse may be
    Thy praise.

Peace

Sweet Peace, where dost thou dwell? I humbly crave,
    Let me once know.
      I sought thee in a secret cave,
        And ask'd if Peace were there.
A hollow winde did seem to answer, 'No;
      Go seek elsewhere.'

I did; and going did a rainbow note:
    Surely, thought I,
      This is the lace of Peace's coat:
        I will search out the matter.
But while I lookt, the clouds immediately
      Did break and scatter.

Then went I to a garden, and did spy
    A gallant flower,
      The Crown Imperiall. Sure, said I,
        Peace at the root must dwell.
But when I digg'd, I saw a worme devoure
      What show'd so well.

At length I met a rev'rend good old man,
    Whom when for Peace
      I did demand, he thus began:
        'There was a Prince of old
At Salem dwelt, Who liv'd with good increase
      Of flock and fold.

'He sweetly liv'd; yet sweetnesse did not save
    His life from foes.
      But after death out of His grave
        There sprang twelve stalks of wheat;
Which many wond'ring at, got some of those
      To plant and set.

'It prosper'd strangely, and did soon disperse
    Through all the earth;
      For they that taste it do rehearse

That vertue lies therein;
A secret vertue, bringing peace and mirth
        By flight of sinne.

'Take of this grain, which in my garden grows,
        And grows for you;
    Make bread of it; and that repose
    And peace, which ev'ry where
With so much earnestnesse you do pursue,
        Is onely there.'

Confession

        O what a cunning guest
Is this same grief! within my heart I made
    Closets, and in them many a chest;
    And like a master in my trade,
In those chests, boxes; in each box a till.
Yet Grief knows all, and enters when he will.

        No scrue, no piercer can
Into a piece of timber worke and winde
    As God's afflictions into man,
    When He a torture hath design'd;
They are too subtill for the subt'llest hearts,
And fall like rheumes upon the tendrest parts.

        We are the earth; and they,
    Like moles within us, heave and cast about;
        And till they foot and clutch their prey,
        They never cool, much lesse give out.
    No smith can make such locks but they have keyes;
    Closets are halls to them, and hearts high-wayes.

        Onely an open breast
Doth shut them out, so that they cannot enter;
        Or if they enter, cannot rest,
        But quickly seek some new adventure:
    Smooth open hearts no fastning have; but fiction
    Doth give a hold and handle to affliction.

Wherefore my faults and sinnes,
Lord, I acknowledge; take Thy plagues away:
For since confession pardon winnes,
I challenge here the brightest day,
The clearest diamond; let them do their best,
They shall be thick and cloudie to my breast.

Giddinesse

Oh, what a thing is man! how farre from power,
From settled peace and rest!
He is some twentie sev'rall men at least
Each sev'rall houre.

One while he counts of heav'n, as of his treasure;
But then a thought creeps in,
And calls him coward, who for fear of sinne
Will lose a pleasure.

Now he will fight it out, and to the warres;
Now eat his bread in peace,
And snudge in quiet; now he scorns increase,
Now all day spares.

He builds a house, which quickly down must go,
As if a whirlwinde blew
And crusht the building; and it's partly true
His minde is so.

O, what a sight were man, if his attires
Did alter with his minde,
And, like a dolphin's skinne, his clothes combin'd
With his desires!

Surely if each one saw another's heart,
There would be no commerce,
No sale or bargain passe; all would disperse
And live apart.

Lord, mend, or rather make us; one creation
Will not suffice our turn:
Except Thou make us dayly, we shall spurn
Our own salvation.

The Bunch of Grapes

Joy, I did lock thee up, but some bad man
    Hath let thee out again;
And now, methinks, I am where I began
    Sev'n years ago: one vogue and vein,
    One aire of thoughts usurps my brain.
I did toward Canaan draw, but now I am
Brought back to the Red Sea, the sea of shame.

For as the Jews of old by God's command
    Travell'd and saw no town,
So now each Christian hath his journeys spann'd;
    Their storie pennes and sets us down.
    A single deed is small renown;
God's works are wide, and let in future times;
His ancient justice overflows our crimes.

Then have we too our guardian fires and clouds,
    Our Scripture-dew drops fast;
We have our sands and serpents, tents and shrowds;
    Alas, our murmurings come not last!
    But where's the cluster? where's the taste
Of mine inheritance? Lord, if I must borrow,
Let me as well take up their joy as sorrow.

But can he want the grape who hath the wine?
    I have their fruit and more.
Blessèd be God, Who prosper'd Noah's vine,
    And made it bring forth grapes, good store:
    But much more Him I must adore
Who of the Law's sowre juice sweet wine did make,
Ev'n God Himself being pressèd for my sake.

Love-Unknown

Deare friend, sit down; the tale is long and sad;
And in my faintings I presume your love
Will more complie then help: – a Lord I had,
And have, of Whom some grounds, which may improve,
I hold for two lives, and both lives in me.
To Him I brought a dish of fruit one day,
And in the middle plac'd my heart. But He,
                       I sigh to say,
Lookt on a servant, who did know His eye
Better then you know me, or, which is one,
Then I, myself. The servant instantly
Quitting the fruit, seiz'd on my heart alone,
And threw it in a font, wherein did fall
A stream of bloud, which issu'd from the side
Of a great rock: – I well remember all,
And have good cause: – there it was dipt and dy'd,
And washt and wrung; the very wringing yet
Enforceth tears. 'Your heart was foul, I fear.'
Indeed 'tis true: I did and do commit
Many a fault more then my lease will bear:
Yet still askt pardon, and was not deni'd.
But you shall heare. After my heart was well,
And clean and fair, as I one even-tide,
                       I sigh to tell,
Walkt by myself abroad, I saw a large
And spacious fornace flaming, and thereon
A boyling caldron, round about whose verge
Was in great letters set 'Affliction'.
The greatnesse shew'd the owner. So I went
To fetch a sacrifice out of my fold,
Thinking with that which I did thus present
To warm His love, which I did fear grew cold.
But as my heart did tender it, the man
Who was to take it from me, slipt his hand,
And threw my heart into the scalding pan;
My heart that brought it (do you understand?),
The offerer's heart. 'Your heart was hard, I fear.'
Indeed 'tis true. I found a callous matter

Began to spread and to expatiate there:
But with a richer drug then scalding water
I bath'd it often, ev'n with holy bloud,
Which at a board, while many drank bare wine,
A friend did steal into my cup for good,
Ev'n taken inwardly, and most divine
To supple hardnesses. But at the length
Out of the caldron getting, soon I fled
Unto my house, where, to repair the strength
Which I had lost, I hasted to my bed:
But when I thought to sleep out all these faults,
                        I sigh to speak,
I found that some had stuff'd the bed with thoughts,
I would say thorns. Deare, could my heart not break,
When with my pleasures ev'n my rest was gone?
Full well I understood who had been there,
For I had giv'n the key to none but one:
It must be He. 'Your heart was dull, I fear.'
Indeed a slack and sleepie state of minde
Did oft possesse me; so that when I pray'd,
Though my lips went, my heart did stay behinde.
But all my scores were by another paid,
Who took the debt upon Him. 'Truly, friend,
For ought I heare, your Master shows to you
More favour then you wot of. Mark the end.
The Font did onely what was old renew;
The Caldron suppled what was grown too hard;
The Thorns did quicken what was grown too dull:
All did but strive to mend what you had marr'd.
Wherefore be cheer'd, and praise Him to the full
Each day, each houre, each moment of the week,
Who fain would have you be new, tender, quick.'

Man's Medley

Heark how the birds do sing,
    And woods do ring:
All creatures have their joy, and man hath his.
    Yet if we rightly measure,
    Man's joy and pleasure
Rather hereafter then in present is.

To this life things of sense
    Make their pretence;
In th' other angels have a right by birth:
    Man ties them both alone,
    And makes them one,
With th' one hand touching heav'n, with th' other earth.

In soul he mounts and flies,
    in flesh he dies;
He wears a stuffe whose thread is course and round,
    But trimm'd with curious lace,
    And should take place
After the trimming, not the stuffe and ground.

Not that he may not here
    Taste of the cheer;
But as birds drink, and straight lift up their head,
    So must he sip and think
    Of better drink
He may attain to after he is dead.

But as his joyes are double,
    So is his trouble:
He hath two winters, other things but one;
    Both frosts and thoughts do nip
    And bite his lip;
And he of all things fears two deaths alone.

Yet ev'n the greatest griefs
    May be reliefs,
Could he but take them right and in their wayes.
    Happie is he whose heart
    Hath found the art
To turn his double pains to double praise.

The Storm

If as the windes and waters here below
      Do flie and flow,
My sighs and tears as busie were above,
      Sure they would move
And much affect Thee, as tempestuous times
Amaze poore mortals, and object their crimes.

Starres have their storms even in a high degree,
      As well as we:
A throbbing conscience spurrèd by remorse
      Hath a strange force;
It quits the earth, and mounting more and more,
Dares to assault Thee, and besiege Thy doore.

There it stands knocking, to Thy musick's wrong,
      And drowns the song:
Glorie and honour are set by till it
      An answer get.
Poets have wrong'd poore storms: such dayes are best,
They purge the aire without; within, the breast.

Paradise

I blesse Thee, Lord, because I GROW
Among Thy trees, which in a ROW
To Thee both fruit and order OW.

What open force or hidden CHARM
Can blast my fruit, or bring me HARM,
While the inclosure is Thine ARM?

Inclose me still, for fear I START;
Be to me rather sharp and TART
Then let me want Thy hand and ART

When Thou dost greater judgements Spare,
And with Thy knife but prune and Pare,
Ev'n fruitful trees more fruitfull Are:

Such sharpnes shows the sweetest Frend,
Such cuttings rather heal then Rend,
And such beginnings touch their End.

The Method

Poore heart, lament;
For since thy God refuseth still,
There is some rub, some discontent,
   Which cools His will.

Thy Father could
Quickly effect what thou dost move,
For He is power; and sure He would,
   For He is Love.

Go search this thing,
Tumble thy breast, and turn thy book:
If thou hadst lost a glove or ring,
   Wouldst thou not look?

What do I see
Written above there? 'Yesterday
I did behave me carelessly
   When I did pray.'

And should God's eare
To such indifferents chainèd be,
Who do not their own motions heare?
   Is God lesse free?

But stay! – what's there?
'Late when I would have something done
I had a motion to forbear,
   Yet I went on.'

And should God's care,
Which needs not man, be ty'd to those
Who heare not Him, but quickly heare
His utter foes?

Then once more pray:
Down with thy knees, up with thy voice;
Seek pardon first, and God will say,
'Glad heart, rejoyce.'

Divinitie

As men, for fear the starres should sleep and nod
And trip at night, have spheres suppli'd, –
As if a starre were duller then a clod,
Which knows his way without a guide, –

Just so the other heav'n they also serve,
Divinitie's transcendent skie,
Which with the edge of wit they cut and carve:
Reason triumphs, and Faith lies by.

Could not that wisdome, which first broacht the wine,
Have thicken'd it with definitions?
And jagg'd His seamlesse coat, had that been fine,
With curious questions and divisions?

But all the doctrine which He taught and gave,
Was cleare as heav'n, from whence it came;
At least those beams of truth, which onely save,
Surpasse in brightnesse any flame.

'Love God' and 'Love your neighbour,' 'Watch and pray,'
'Do as you would be done unto';
O dark instructions, ev'n as dark as day!
Who can these Gordian knots undo!

'But He doth bid us take His bloud for wine.'
Bid what He please; yet I am sure,
To take and taste what He doth there designe
Is all that saves, and not obscure.

Then burn thy epicycles, foolish man,
    Break all thy spheres, and save thy head;
Faith needs no staffe of flesh, but stoutly can
    To heav'n alone both go and leade.

Grieve Not the Holy Spirit

Ephesians iv: 30

And art Thou grievèd, sweet and sacred Dove,
    When I am sowre,
    And crosse Thy love?
Grievèd for me? the God of strength and power
    Griev'd for a worm, which, when I tread,
    I passe away and leave it dead?

Then weep, mine eyes, the God of love doth grieve;
    Weep, foolish heart,
    And weeping live;
For death is drie as dust. Yet if ye part
    End as the night, whose sable hue
    Your sinnes expresse, melt into dew.

When sawcie Mirth shall knock or call at doore,
    Cry out, 'Get hence,
    Or cry no more!'
Almightie God doth grieve, He puts on sense;
    I sinne not to my grief alone,
    But to my God's too; He doth grone.

O, take thy lute, and tune it to a strain
    Which may with thee
    All day complain;
There can no discord but in ceasing be.
    Marble can weep, and surely strings
    More bowels have then such hard things.

Lord, I adjudge myself to tears and grief,
    Ev'n endlesse tears
    Without relief;

If a cleare spring for me no time forbears,
    But runnes, although I be not drie –
    I am no crystall – what shall I?

Yet if I wail not still, since still to wail
      Nature denies,
      And flesh would fail;
If my deserts were masters of mine eyes, –
    Lord, pardon, for Thy Sonne makes good
    My want of tears with store of bloud.

The Familie

What doth this noise of thoughts within my heart,
    As if they had a part?
What do these loud complaints and puling fears,
    As if there were no rule or eares?

But, Lord, the house and familie are Thine,
    Though some of them repine;
Turn out these wranglers, which defile Thy seat,
    For where Thou dwellest all is neat.

First Peace and Silence all disputes controll,
    Then Order plaies the soul;
And giving all things their set forms and houres,
    Makes of wilde woods sweet walks and bowres.

Humble Obedience neare the doore doth stand,
    Expecting a command;
Then whom in waiting, nothing seems more slow,
    Nothing more quick when she doth go.

Joyes oft are there, and griefs as oft as joyes;
    But griefs without a noise:
Yet speak they louder then distemper'd fears;
    What is so shrill as silent tears?

This is Thy house, with these it doth abound;
    And where these are not found
Perhaps Thou com'st sometimes, and for a day;
    But not to make a constant stay.

The Size

Content thee, greedie heart;
Modest and moderate joyes to those that have
Title to more hereafter when they part
    Are passing brave.
    Let th' upper springs into the low
    Descend and fall, and thou dost flow.

What though some have a fraught
Of cloves and nutmegs, and in cinnamon sail?
If thou hast wherewithall to spice a draught
    When griefs prevail,
    And, for the future time, art heir
    To th' Isle of spices, is't not fair?

To be in both worlds full
Is more then God was, Who was hungrie here.
Wouldst thou His laws of feasting disanull;
    Enact good cheer?
    Lay out thy joy, yet hope to save it?
    Wouldst thou both eat thy cake, and have it?

Great joyes are all at once;
But little do reserve themselves for more:
Those have their hopes, these what they have renounce,
    And live on score;
    Those are at home; these journey still,
    And meet the rest on Sion's hill.

Thy Saviour sentenc'd joy,
And in the flesh condemn'd it as unfit;
At least in lump, for such doth oft destroy;
    Whereas a bit
    Doth 'tice us on to hopes of more,
    And for the present, health restore.

A Christian's state and case
Is not a corpulent, but a thinne and spare,
Yet active strength; whose long and bonie face
    Content and care
    Do seem to equally divide,
    Like a pretender, not a bride.

Wherefore sit down, good heart;
Grasp not at much, for fear thou losest all.
If comforts fell according to desert, –

*

They would great frosts and snows destroy:
For we should count, – Since the last joy.

Then close again the seam
Which thou hast open'd; do not spread thy robe
In hopes of great things. Call to minde thy dream,
    An earthly globe,
    On whose meridian was engraven,
    'These seas are tears, and Heav'n the haven.'

Artillerie

As I one evening sat before my cell,
Me thought a starre did shoot into my lap.
I rose, and shook my clothes, as knowing well
That from small fires comes oft no small mishap;
    When suddenly I heard one say,
    'Do as thou usest, disobey,
    Expell good motions from thy breast,
Which have the face of fire, but end in rest.'

I, who had heard of music in the spheres,
But not of speech in starres, began to muse;
But turning to my God, Whose ministers
The starres and all things are: 'If I refuse,
    Dread Lord,' said I, 'so oft my good,
    Then I refuse not ev'n with bloud
    To wash away my stubborn thought;
For I will do, or suffer what I ought.'

But I have also starres and shooters too,
Born where Thy servants both artilleries use:
My tears and prayers night and day do woo,
And work up to Thee; yet Thou dost refuse.
    Not but I am (I must say still)

Much more oblig'd to do Thy will
Than Thou to grant mine; but because
Thy promise now hath ev'n set Thee Thy laws.

Then we are shooters both, and Thou dost deigne
To enter combate with us, and contest
With Thine own clay. But I would parley fain:
Shunne not my arrows, and behold my breast.
   Yet if Thou shunnest, I am Thine,
   I must be so, if I am mine: –
   There is no articling with Thee;
I am but finite, – yet Thine infinitely.

Church-Rents and Schismes

Brave rose, alas, where art thou? In the chair
Where thou didst lately so triumph and shine,
A worm doth sit, whose many feet and hair
Are the more foul, the more thou wert divine.
This, this hath done it, this did bite the root
And bottome of the leaves; which when the winde
Did once perceive, it blew them under foot,
Where rude unhallow'd steps do crush and grinde
   Their beauteous glories. Onely shreds of thee,
   And those all bitten, in thy chair I see.

Why doth my Mother blush? is she the rose,
And shows it so? Indeed Christ's precious bloud
Gave you a colour once; which when your foes
Thought to let out, the bleeding did you good,
And made you look much fresher then before.
But when debates and fretting jealousies
Did worm and work within you more and more,
Your colour faded, and calamities
   Turnèd your ruddie into pale and bleak:
   Your health and beautie both began to break.

Then did your sev'rall parts unloose and start;
Which when your neighbours saw, like a north-winde
They rushèd in, and cast them in the dirt,
Where Pagans tread. O Mother deare and kinde,
Where shall I get me eyes enough to weep –
As many eyes as starres! since it is night,
And much of Asia and Europe fast asleep,
And ev'n all Africk: would at least I might
    With these two poore ones lick up all the dew,
    Which falls by night, and poure it out for you!

Justice

O dreadfull justice, what a fright and terrour
        Wast thou of old,
        When Sinne and Errour
    Did show and shape thy looks to me,
    And through their glasse discolour thee!
He that did but look up was proud and bold.

The dishes of thy balance seem'd to gape,
        Like two great pits;
        The beam and 'scape
    Did like some tort'ring engine show:
    Thy hand above did burn and glow,
Daunting the stoutest hearts, the proudest wits.

But now that Christ's pure vail presents the sight,
        I see no fears:
        Thy hand is white,
    Thy scales like buckets, which attend
    And interchangeably descend,
Lifting to heaven from this well of tears.

For where before thou still didst call on me,
        Now I still touch
        And harp on thee;
    God's promises have made thee mine:
    Why should I justice now decline?
Against me there is none, but for me much.

The Pilgrimage

I travell'd on, seeing the hill, where lay
                    My expectation.
        A long it was and weary way:
        The gloomy cave of Desperation
I left on th' one, and on the other side
                    The rock of Pride.

And so I came to Phansie's medow strow'd
                    With many a flower:
        Fain would I here have made abode,
        But I was quicken'd by my houre.
So to Care's cops I came, and there got through
                    With much ado.

That led me to the wilde of Passion, which
                    Some call the wold;
        A wasted place, but sometimes rich.
        Here I was robb'd of all my gold,
Save one good angell, which a friend had ti'd
                    Close to my side.

At length I got unto the gladsome hill,
                    Where lay my hope,
        Where lay my heart; and climbing still,
        When I had gain'd the brow and top,
A lake of brackish waters on the ground
                    Was all I found.

With that abash'd and struck with many a sting
                    Of swarming fears,
        I fell and cry'd, 'Alas, my King,
        Can both the way and end be tears?'
Yet taking heart I rose, and then perceiv'd
                    I was deceiv'd,

My hill was further; so I flung away,
                    Yet heard a crie,
        Just as I went, 'None goes that way
        And lives.' 'If that be all,' said I,
'After so foul a journey death is fair,
                    And but a chair.'

The Holdfast

I threatened to observe the strict decree
  Of my deare God with all my power and might:
But I was told by one, 'It could not be;
  Yet I might trust in God to be my light.'

'Then will I trust,' said I, 'in Him alone.'
  'Nay, ev'n to trust in Him, was also His:
We must confesse that nothing is our own.'
  'Then I confesse that He my succour is.'

'But to have nought is ours, not to confesse
  That we have nought.' I stood amaz'd at this,
Much troubled, till I heard a friend expresse
  That all things were more ours by being His:

What Adam had, and forfeited for all,
Christ keepeth now, Who cannot fail or fall.

Complaining

Do not beguile my heart,
     Because Thou art
My power and wisdome. Put me not to shame
     Because I am
Thy clay that weeps, Thy dust that calls.

Thou art the Lord of glorie;
     The deed and storie
Are both Thy due: but I a silly flie,
     That live or die
According as the weather falls.

Art Thou all justice, Lord?
     Shows not Thy Word
More attributes? Am I all throat or eye,
     To weep or crie?
Have I no parts but those of grief?

Let not Thy wrathfull power
    Afflict my houre,
My inch of life; or let Thy gracious power
     Contract my houre,
  That I may climbe and finde relief.

The Discharge

Busie enquiring heart, what would'st thou know?
    Why dost thou prie,
And turn, and leer, and with a licorous eye
    Look high and low,
  And in thy lookings stretch and grow?

Hast thou not made thy counts, and summ'd up all?
    Did not thy heart
Give up the whole, and with the whole depart?
    Let what will fall,
  That which is past who can recall?

Thy life is God's, thy time to come is gone,
    And is His right.
He is thy night at noon; He is at night
    Thy noon alone;
  The crop is His, for He hath sown.

And well it was for thee, when this befell,
    That God did make
Thy businesse His, and in thy life partake;
    For thou canst tell,
  If it be His once, all is well.

Onely the present is thy part and fee;
    And happy thou
If, though thou didst not beat thy future brow,
    Thou could'st well see
  What present things requir'd of thee.

They ask enough; why shouldst thou further go?
      Raise not the mudde
Of future depths, but drink the cleare and good:
      Dig not for wo
    In times to come, for it will grow.

Man and the present fit; if he provide,
      He breaks the square.
This houre is mine: if for the next I care,
      I grow too wide,
    And do encroach upon Death's side;

For Death each hour environs and surrounds.
      He that would know
And care for future chances cannot go
      Unto those grounds
    But through a churchyard which them bounds.

Things present shrink and die; but they that spend
      Their thoughts and sense
On future grief do not remove it thence,
      But it extend,
    And draw the bottome out an end.

God chains the dog till night; wilt loose the chain,
      And wake thy sorrow?
Wilt thou forestall it, and now grieve to-morrow,
      And then again
    Grieve over freshly all thy pain?

Either grief will not come, or if it must,
      Do not forecast;
And while it cometh it is almost past.
      Away, distrust;
    My God hath promis'd; He is just.

Praise

King of glorie, King of peace,
    I will love Thee;
And, that love may never cease,
    I will move Thee.

Thou hast granted my request,
    Thou hast heard me;
Thou didst note my working breast,
    Thou hast spar'd me.

Wherefore with my utmost art
    I will sing Thee,
And the cream of all my heart
    I will bring Thee.

Though my sins against me cried,
    Thou didst cleare me;
And alone, when they replied,
    Thou didst heare me.

Sev'n whole dayes, not one in seven,
    I will praise Thee;
In my heart, though not in heaven,
    I can raise Thee.

Thou grew'st soft and moist with tears,
    Thou relentedst,
And when Justice call'd for fears,
    Thou dissentedst.

Small it is in this poore sort
    To enroll Thee;
Ev'n eternitie is too short
    To extoll Thee.

An Offering

Come, bring thy gift. If blessings were as slow
As men's returns, what would become of fools?
What hast thou there – a heart? but is it pure?
Search well, and see, for hearts have many holes.
Yet one pure heart is nothing to bestow;
In Christ two natures met to be thy cure.

O, that within us hearts had propagation,
Since many gifts do challenge many hearts!
Yet one, if good, may title to a number,
And single things grow fruitfull by deserts.
In public judgments one may be a nation,
And fence a plague, while others sleep and slumber.

But all I fear is, lest thy heart displease,
As neither good nor one; so oft divisions
Thy lusts have made, and not thy lusts alone –
Thy passions also have their set partitions:
These parcell out thy heart; recover these,
And thou mayst offer many gifts in one.

There is a balsome, or indeed a bloud,
Dropping from heav'n, which doth both cleanse and close
All sorts of wounds, of such strange force it is.
Seek out this All-heal, and seek no repose
Untill thou finde, and use it to thy good:
Then bring thy gift, and let thy hymne be this:

Since my sadnesse
Into gladnesse,
Lord, Thou dost convert;
O, accept
What Thou hast kept
As Thy due desert.

Had I many,
Had I any –
For this heart is none –

        All were Thine,
        And none of mine;
    Surely Thine alone.

        Yet Thy favour
        May give savour
    To this poore oblation,
        And it raise
        To be Thy praise,
    And be my salvation.

Longing

    With sick and famisht eyes,
    With doubling knees, and weary bones,
        To Thee my cries,
        To Thee my grones,
    To Thee my sighs, my tears ascend
        No end?

    My throat, my soul is hoarse;
    My heart is wither'd like a ground
        Which Thou dost curse;
        My thoughts turn round,
    And make me giddie: Lord, I fall,
        Yet call.

    From Thee all pitie flows:
    Mothers are kinde because Thou art,
        And dost dispose
        To them a part:
    Their infants, them, and they suck Thee
        More free.

    Bowels of pitie, heare;
    Lord of my soul, love of my minde,
        Bow down Thine eare;
        Let not the winde
    Scatter my words, and in the same
        Thy name.

Look on my sorrows round;
Mark well my furnace. O, what flames,
    What heats abound!
    What griefs, what shames!
Consider, Lord; Lord, bow Thine eare,
        And heare.

Lord Jesu, Thou didst bow
Thy dying head upon the tree;
    O, be not now
    More dead to me.
Lord, heare. 'Shall He that made the eare
        Not heare?'

Behold, Thy dust doth stirre;
It moves, it creeps, it aims at Thee;
    Wilt Thou deferre
    To succour me,
Thy pile of dust, wherein each crumme
        Sayes, Come?

To Thee help appertains;
Hast Thou left all things to their course,
    And laid the reins
    Upon the horse?
Is all lockt? hath a sinner's plea
        No key?

Indeed, the world's Thy book,
Where all things have their leaf assign'd;
    Yet a meek look
    Hath interlin'd:
Thy board is full, yet humble guests
        Finde nests.

Thou tarriest, while I die,
And fall to nothing: Thou dost reign
    And rule on high,
    While I remain
In bitter grief; yet am I stil'd
        Thy childe.

Lord, didst Thou leave Thy throne
Not to relieve? how can it be
    That Thou art grown
    Thus hard to me?
Were sinne alive, good cause there were
    To bear:

But now both sinne is dead,
And all Thy promises live and bide;
    That wants his head,
    These speak and chide,
And in Thy bosome poure my tears,
    As theirs.

Lord JESU, heare my heart,
Which hath been broken now so long,
    That ev'ry part
    Hath got a tongue:
Thy beggars grow; rid them away
    To-day.

My Love, my Sweetnesse, heare:
By these Thy feet, at which my heart
    Lies all the yeare,
    Pluck out Thy dart,
And heal my troubled breast, which cries,
    Which dies.

The Bag

Away, despair! my gracious Lord doth heare;
  Though windes and waves assault my keel,
  He doth preserve it; He doth steer
  Ev'n when the boat seems most to reel.
  Storms are the triumph of His art;
Well may He close His eyes, but not His heart.

Hast thou not heard that my Lord Jesus di'd?
  Then let me tell thee a strange storie:

The God of power, as He did ride
   In His majestick robes of glorie,
   Resolv'd to 'light; and so one day
He did descend, undressing all the way.

The starres His tire of light and rings obtain'd,
   The cloud His bow, the fire His spear,
   The sky His azure mantle gain'd;
   And when they ask'd what He would wear,
   He smil'd, and said as He did go,
He had new clothes a-making here below.

When He was come, as travellers are wont,
   He did repair unto an inne.
   Both then, and after, many a brunt
   He did endure to cancell sinne;
   And having giv'n the rest before,
Here He gave up His life to pay our score.

But as He was returning, there came one
   That ran upon Him with a spear.
   He, who came hither all alone,
   Bringing nor man, nor arms, nor fear,
   Receiv'd the blow upon His side,
And straight He turn'd, and to His brethren cry'd,

'If ye have anything to send or write –
   I have no bag, but here is room –
   Unto My Father's hands and sights
   Beleeve Me, it shall safely come.
   That I shall minde what you impart,
Look, you may put it very neare My heart.

'Or if hereafter any of My friends
   Will use Me in this kinde, the doore
   Shall still be open; what he sends
   I will present, and somewhat more,
   Not to his hurt: sighs will convey
Anything to Me.' Heark, Despair, away!

The Jews

Poore nation, whose sweet sap and juice
Our cyens have purloin'd and left you drie;
Whose streams we got by the Apostles' sluce,
And use in baptisme, while ye pine and die;
Who by not keeping once, became a debter,
    And now by keeping lose the letter; –

Oh that my prayers – mine, alas!
Oh that some angel might a trumpet sound,
At which the Church, falling upon her face,
Should crie so loud untill the trump were drown'd,
And by that crie, of her deare Lord obtain
    That your sweet sap might come again!

The Collar

I struck the board, and cry'd, 'No more;
    I will abroad.'
  What, shall I ever sigh and pine?
My lines and life are free; free as the road,
  Loose as the winde, as large as store.
    Shall I be still in suit?
  Have I no harvest but a thorn
  To let me bloud, and not restore
  What I have lost with cordiall fruit?
    Sure there was wine
  Before my sighs did drie it; there was corn
    Before my tears did drown it;
  Is the yeare onely lost to me?
    Have I no bayes to crown it,
No flowers, no garlands gay? all blasted,
    All wasted?
  Not so, my heart; but there is fruit,
    And thou hast hands.
  Recover all thy sigh-blown age
On double pleasures; leave thy cold dispute
Of what is fit and not; forsake thy cage,

Thy rope of sands
Which pettie thoughts have made; and made to thee
Good cable, to enforce and draw,
And be thy law,
While thou didst wink and wouldst not see.
Away! take heed;
I will abroad.
Call in thy death's-head there, tie up thy fears;
He that forbears
To suit and serve his need
Deserves his load.
But as I rav'd and grew more fierce and wilde
At every word,
Methought I heard one calling, 'Childe';
And I reply'd, 'My Lord.'

The Glimpse

Whither away, Delight?
Thou cam'st but now; wilt thou so soon depart,
And give me up to night?
For many weeks of lingring pain and smart,
But one half houre of comfort for my heart!

Methinks Delight should have
More skill in musick, and keep better time.
Wert thou a winde or wave,
They quickly go and come with lesser crime;
Flowrs look about, and die not in their prime.

Thy short abode and stay
Feeds not, but addes to the desire of meat.
Lime begg'd of old, they say,
A neighbour spring to cool his inward heat,
Which by the spring's accesse grew much more great.

In hope of thee, my heart
Pickt here and there a crumme, and would not die;
   But constant to his part,
When-as my fears foretold this, did replie,
A slender thread a gentle guest will tie.

   Yet if the heart that wept
Must let thee go, return when it doth knock.
   Although thy heap be kept
For future times, the droppings of the stock
May oft break forth, and never break the lock.

   If I have more to spinne,
The wheel shall go, so that thy stay be short.
   Thou knowst how grief and sinne
Disturb the work. O, make me not their sport,
Who by Thy coming may be made a Court!

Assurance

   O spitefull bitter thought,
Bitterly spitefull thought! Couldst thou invent
So high a torture? is such poyson bought?
Doubtlesse, but in the way of punishment;
   When wit contrives to meet with thee,
   No such rank poyson can there be.

   Thou saidst but even now
That all was not so fair as I conceiv'd
Betwixt my God and me. That I allow,
And coin large hopes, but that I was deceiv'd:
   Either the league was broke, or neare it;
   And that I had great cause to fear it.

   And what to this? what more
Could poyson, if it had a tongue, expresse?
What is thy aim? wouldst thou unlock the doore
To cold despairs and gnawing pensivenesse?
   Wouldst thou raise devils? I see, I know;
   I writ thy purpose long ago.

But I will to my Father,
Who heard thee say it. O most gracious Lord,
If all the hope and comfort that I gather
Were from myself, I had not half a word,
   Not half a letter to oppose
   What is objected by my foes.

   But Thou art my desert:
And in this league, which now my foes invade,
Thou art not onely to perform Thy part,
But also mine; as when the league was made,
   Thou didst at once Thyself indite,
   And hold my hand while I did write.

   Wherefore, if Thou canst fail,
Then can Thy truth and I: but while rocks stand
And rivers stirre, Thou canst not shrink or quail;
Yea, when both rocks and all things shall disband,
   Then shalt Thou be my rock and tower,
   And make their ruine praise Thy power.

   Now, foolish thought, go on,
Spin out thy thread, and make thereof a coat
To hide thy shame; for thou hast cast a bone
Which bounds on thee, and will not down thy throat:
   What for it self Love once began,
   Now Love and Truth will end in man.

The Call

Come, my Way, my Truth, my Life!
Such a Way as gives us breath,
Such a Truth as ends all strife,
Such a Life as killeth Death.

Come, my Light, my Feast, my Strength!
Such a Light as shows a feast,
Such a Feast as mends in length,
Such a Strength as makes his guest.

Come, my Joy, my Love, my Heart!
Such a Joy as none can move,
Such a Love as none can part,
Such a Heart as joyes in love.

Clasping of Hands

Lord, Thou art mine, and I am Thine,
If mine I am; and Thine much more
Than I or ought or can be mine.
Yet to be Thine doth me restore,
So that again I now am mine,
And with advantage mine the more,
Since this being mine brings with it Thine,
And Thou with me dost Thee restore:
    If I without Thee would be mine,
    I neither should be mine nor Thine.

Lord, I am Thine, and Thou art mine;
So mine Thou art, that something more
I may presume Thee mine then Thine,
For Thou didst suffer to restore
Not Thee, but me, and to be mine:
And with advantage mine the more,
Since Thou in death wast none of Thine,
Yet then as mine didst me restore:
    O, be mine still; still make me Thine
    Or rather make no Thine and mine.

Praise

Lord, I will mean and speak Thy praise,
    Thy praise alone;
My busie heart shall spin it all my dayes;
    And when it stops for want of store,
Then will I wring it with a sigh or grone
    That Thou mayst yet have more.

When Thou dost favour any action,
    It runnes, it flies;
All things concurre to give it a perfection.
    That which had but two legs before,
When Thou dost blesse, hath twelve; one wheel doth rise
    To twentie then, or more.

But when Thou dost on businesse blow,
    It hangs, it clogs;
Not all the teams of Albion in a row
    Can hale or draw it out of doore:
Legs are but stumps, and Pharaoh's wheels but logs,
    And struggling hinders more.

Thousands of things do Thee employ
    In ruling all
This spacious globe: angels must have their joy,
    Devils their rod, the sea his shore,
The windes their stint: and yet when I did call,
    Thou heardst my call, and more.

I have not lost one single tear;
    But when mine eyes
Did weep to heav'n, they found a bottle there –
    As we have boxes for the poor –
Readie to take them in; yet of a size
    That would contain much more.

But after Thou hadst slipt a drop
  From Thy right eye –
Which there did hang like streamers neare the top
  Of some fair church, to show the sore
And bloudie battell which Thou once didst trie –
  The glasse was full and more.

Wherefore I sing. Yet since my heart
  Though press'd, runnes thin;
O that I might some other hearts convert,
  And so take up at use good store;
That to Thy chests there might be coming in
  Both all my praise, and more!

Joseph's Coat

Wounded I sing, tormented I indite,
Thrown down I fall into a bed and rest:
Sorrow hath chang'd its note; such is His will
Who changeth all things as Him pleaseth best:
  For well He knows, if but one grief and smart
Among my many had his full career,
Sure it would carrie with it ev'n my heart,
And both would runne until they found a biere
  To fetch the bodie, both being due to grief
But He hath spoil'd the race; and giv'n to anguish
One of Joye's coats, 'ticing it with relief
To linger in me, and together languish.
   I live to shew His power, Who once did bring
   My joyes to weep, and now my griefs to sing.

The Pulley

When God at first made man,
Having a glasse of blessings standing by,
'Let us,' said He, 'poure on him all we can;
Let the world's riches, which dispersèd lie,
          Contract into a span.'

So strength first made a way;
Then beautie flow'd, then wisdome, honour, pleasure;
When almost all was out, God made a stay,
Perceiving that, alone of all His treasure,
          Rest in the bottome lay.

'For if I should,' said He,
'Bestow this jewell also on My creature,
He would adore My gifts in stead of Me,
And rest in Nature, not the God of Nature:
          So both should losers be.

'Yet let him keep the rest,
But keep them with repining restlessnesse;
Let him be rich and wearie, that at least,
If goodnesse leade him not, yet wearinesse
          May tosse him to My breast.'

The Priesthood

Blest Order, which in power dost so excell,
That with th' one hand thou liftest to the sky,
And with the other throwest down to hell
In thy just censures; fain would I draw nigh,
Fain put thee on, exchanging my lay-sword
          For that of th' Holy Word.

But thou art fire, sacred and hallow'd fire,
And I but earth and clay; should I presume
To wear thy habit, the severe attire
My slender compositions might consume:
I am both foul and brittle, much unfit
          To deal in Holy Writ.

Yet have I often seen, by cunning hand
And force of fire, what curious things are made
Of wretched earth. Where once I scorn'd to stand,
That earth is fitted, by the fire and trade
Of skilfull artists, for the boards of those
        Who make the bravest shows.

But since those great ones, be they ne're so great,
Come from the earth, from whence those vessels come,
So that at once both feeder, dish, and meat
Have one beginning and one finall summe;
I do not greatly wonder at the sight,
        If earth in earth delight.

But th' holy men of God such vessels are
As serve Him up Who all the world commands.
When God vouchsafeth to become our fare,
Their hands convey Him Who conveys their hands:
O, what pure things, most pure, must those things be
        Who bring my God to me!

Wherefore I dare not, I, put forth my hand
To hold the Ark, although it seem to shake
Through th' old sinnes and new doctrines of our land;
Onely, since God doth often vessels make
Of lowly matter for high uses meet,
        I throw me at His feet.

There will I lie, untill my Maker seek
For some mean stuffe whereon to show His skill;
Then is my time. The distance of the meek
Doth flatter power. Lest good come short of ill
In praising might, the poore do by submission
        What pride by opposition.

The Search

Whither, O whither art Thou fled,
     My Lord, my Love?
My searches are my daily bread,
     Yet never prove.

My knees pierce th' earth, mine eies the skie;
     And yet the sphere
And centre both to me denie
     That Thou art there.

Yet can I mark how herbs below
     Grow green and gay,
As if to meet Thee they did know,
     While I decay.

Yet can I mark how starres above
     Simper and shine,
As having keyes unto Thy love,
     While poore I pine.

I sent a sigh to seek Thee out,
     Deep drawn in pain,
Wing'd like an arrow; but my scout
     Returns in vain.

I tun'd another – having store –
     Into a grone,
Because the search was dumbe before
     But all was one.

Lord, dost Thou some new fabrick mold
     Which favour winnes,
And keeps Thee present; leaving th' old
     Unto their sinnes?

Where is my God? what hidden place
     Conceals Thee still?
What covert dare eclipse Thy face?
     Is it Thy will?

O let not that of any thing;
　　Let rather brasse,
Or steel, or mountains be Thy ring,
　　And I will passe.

Thy will such an intrenching is
　　As passeth thought:
To it all strength, all subtilties
　　Are things of nought.

Thy will such a strange distance is
　　As that to it
East and West touch, the poles do kisse,
　　And parallels meet.

Since, then, my grief must be as large
　　As is Thy space,
Thy distance from me; see my charge,
　　Lord, see my case.

O take these barres, these lengths away;
　　Turn, and restore me:
'Be not Almightie,' let me say,
　　'Against, but for me.'

When Thou dost turn, and wilt be neare,
　　What edge so keen,
What point so piercing can appeare
　　To come between?

For as Thy absence doth excell
　　All distance known,
So doth Thy nearnesse bear the bell,
　　Making two one.

Grief

O who will give me tears? Come, all ye springs,
Dwell in my head and eyes; come, clouds and rain;
My grief hath need of all the wat'ry things
That nature hath produc'd: let ev'ry vein
Suck up a river to supply mine eyes,
My weary weeping eyes, too drie for me,
Unlesse they get new conduits, new supplies,
To bear them out, and with my state agree.
What are two shallow foords, two little spouts
Of a lesse world? the greater is but small,
A narrow cupboard for my griefs and doubts,
Which want provision in the midst of all.
Verses, ye are too fine a thing, too wise,
For my rough sorrows; cease, be dumbe and mute,
Give up your feet and running to mine eyes
And keep your measures for some lover's lute,
Whose grief allows him musick and a ryme;
For mine excludes both measure, tune, and time:
        Alas, my God!

The Crosse

  What is this strange and uncouth thing,
To make me sigh, and seek, and faint, and die,
Untill I had some place where I might sing
    And serve Thee; and not onely I,
But all my wealth and familie might combine
To set Thy honour up as our designe?

  And then when, after much delay,
Much wrastling, many a combate, this deare end,
So much desir'd, is giv'n; to take away
    My power to serve Thee; to unbend
All my abilities, my designes confound,
And lay my threatnings bleeding on the ground.

One ague dwelleth in my bones,
Another in my soul, – the memorie
What I would do for Thee, if once my grones
      Could be allow'd for harmonie; –
I am in all a weak disabled thing,
Save in the sight thereof, where strength doth sting.

      Besides, things sort not to my will
Ev'n when my will doth studie Thy renown:
Thou turnest th' edge of all things on me still,
      Taking me up to throw me down;
So that, ev'n when my hopes seem to be sped,
I am to grief alive, to them as dead.

      To have my aim, and yet to be
Farther from it then when I bent my bow;
To make my hopes my torture, and the fee
      Of all my woes another wo,
Is in the midst of delicates to need,
And ev'n in Paradise to be a weed.

      Ah, my deare Father, ease my smart!
These contrarieties crush me; these crosse actions
Doe winde a rope about, and cut my heart:
      And yet since these Thy contradictions
Are properly a crosse felt by Thy Sonne
With but foure words, my words, 'Thy will be done!'

The Flower

How fresh, O Lord, how sweet and clean
Are Thy returns! ev'n as the flowers in Spring,
   To which, besides their own demean,
The late-past frosts tributes of pleasure bring;
      Grief melts away
      Like snow in May,
   As if there were no such cold thing.

Who would have thought my shrivel'd heart
Could have recover'd greennesse? It was gone
   Quite under ground; as flowers depart
To see their mother-root, when they have blown,
      Where they together
      All the hard weather,
   Dead to the world, keep house unknown.

These are Thy wonders, Lord of power,
Killing and quickning, bringing down to Hell
   And up to Heaven in an houre;
Making a chiming of a passing-bell.
      We say amisse
      This or that is;
   Thy word is all, if we could spell.

O that I once past changing were,
Fast in Thy Paradise, where no flower can wither;
   Many a Spring I shoot up fair,
Offring at Heav'n, growing and groning thither;
      Nor doth my flower
      Want a Spring-showre,
   My sinnes and I joyning together.

But while I grow in a straight line,
Still upwards bent, as if Heav'n were mine own,
   Thy anger comes, and I decline:
What frost to that? what pole is not the zone
      Where all things burn,
      When Thou dost turn,
   And the least frown of Thine is shown?

And now in age I bud again,
After so many deaths I live and write;
    I once more smell the dew and rain,
And relish versing: O, my onely Light,
        It cannot be
        That I am he
    On whom Thy tempests fell all night.

These are Thy wonders, Lord of love,
To make us see we are but flow'rs that glide;
    Which when we once can find and prove,
Thou hast a garden for us where to bide;
        Who would be more,
        Swelling through store,
    Forfeit their Paradise by their pride.

Dotage

False glozing pleasures, casks of happinesse,
Foolish night-fires, women's and children's wishes,
Chases in arras, guilded emptinesse,
Shadows well mounted, dreams in a career,
Embroider'd lyes, nothing between two dishes:
        These are the pleasures here.

True earnest sorrows, rooted miseries,
Anguish in grain, vexations ripe and blown,
Sure-footed griefs, solid calamities,
Plain demonstrations, evident and cleare,
Fetching their proofs ev'n from the very bone:
        These are the sorrows here.

But O the folly of distracted men!
Who griefs in earnest, joyes in jest pursue,
Preferring, like brute beasts, a lothsome den
Before a Court, ev'n that above so cleare,
Where are no sorrows, but delights more true
        Then miseries are here!

The Sonne

Let forrain nations of their language boast
What fine varietie each tongue affords;
I like our language, as our men and coast;
Who cannot dresse it well, want wit, not words.
How neatly do we give one onely name
To parents' issue and the sunne's bright starre!
A sonne is light and fruit; a fruitfull flame
Chasing the father's dimnesse, carried far
From the first man in the East to fresh and new
Western discov'ries of posteritie.
So in one word our Lord's humilitie
We turn upon Him in a sense most true;
    For what Christ once in humblenesse began,
    We Him in glorie call The Sonne of Man.

A True Hymne

    My Joy, my Life, my Crown!
    My heart was meaning all the day,
      Somewhat it fain would say,
And still it runneth mutt'ring up and down
With only this, My Joy, my Life, my Crown!

    Yet slight not these few words;
    If truly said, they may take part
      Among the best in art:
The finenesse which a hymne or psalme affords
Is when the soul into the lines accords.

    He who craves all the minde,
    And all the soul, and strength, and time
      If the words onely ryme,
Justly complains that somewhat is behinde
To make his verse, or write a hymne in kinde.

Whereas, if th' heart be moved,
Although the verse be somewhat scant,
God doth supplie the want;
As when th' heart sayes, sighing to be approved,
'O could I love!' and stops, God writeth 'Loved.'

The Answer

My comforts drop and melt away like snow;
I shake my head, and all the thoughts and ends
Which my fierce youth did bandie, fall and flow
Like leaves about me, or like summer-friends,
Flyes of estates and sunne-shine. But to all
Who think me eager, hot, and undertaking,
But in my prosecutions slack and small;
As a young exhalation, newly waking,
Scorns his first bed of dirt, and means the sky,
But cooling by the way, grows pursie and slow
And setling to a cloud, doth live and die
In that dark state of tears, – to all that so
Show me and set me, I have one reply,
Which they that know the rest know more then I.

A Dialogue-Antheme

Christian   Death

Christian
Alas, poore Death, where is thy glorie?
Where is thy famous force, thy ancient sting?

Death
Alas, poore mortall, void of storie,
Go spell and reade how I have kill'd thy King.

Christian
Poore Death! and who was hurt thereby?
Thy curse being laid on Him makes thee accurst.

Death
Let losers talk, yet thou shalt die;
These arms shall crush thee.

Christian
          Spare not, do thy worst:
I shall be one day better then before;
Thou so much worse, that thou shalt be no more.

The Water-Course

Thou who dost dwell and linger here below,
Since the condition of this world is frail,
Where of all plants afflictions soonest grow,
If troubles overtake thee, do not wail;

For who can look for lesse that loveth $\left\{ \begin{array}{l} \text{Life?} \\ \text{Strife?} \end{array} \right.$

But rather turn the pipe and water's course
To serve thy sinnes, and furnish thee with store
Of sov'raigne tears, springing from true remorse;
That so in purenesse thou mayst Him adore

Who gives to man, as He sees fit, $\left\{ \begin{array}{l} \text{Salvation.} \\ \text{Damnation.} \end{array} \right.$

Self-Condemnation

Thou who condemnest Jewish hate
For choosing Barabbas a murderer
          Before the Lord of glorie,
Look back upon thine own estate,
Call home thine eye, that busie wanderer,
          That choice may be thy storie.

He that doth love, and love amisse,
This world's delights before true Christian joy,
          Hath made a Jewish choice:
The World an ancient murderer is;
Thousands of souls it hath and doth destroy
          With her enchanting voice.

He that hath made a sorrie wedding
Between his soul and gold, and hath preferr'd
    False gain before the true,
    Hath done what he condemnes in reading;
For he hath sold for money his deare Lord,
    And is a Judas-Jew.

    Thus we prevent the last great day,
And judge our selves. That light which sin and passion
    Did before dimme and choke,
    When once those snuffes are ta'ne away,
Shines bright and cleare, ev'n unto condemnation,
    Without excuse or cloke.

Bitter-Sweet

    Ah, my deare angrie Lord,
    Since Thou dost love, yet strike;
    Cast down, yet help afford;
    Sure I will do the like.

    I will complain, yet praise,
    I will bewail, approve;
    And all my sowre-sweet dayes
    I will lament, and love.

The Glance

    When first Thy sweet and gracious eye
Vouchsaf'd, ev'n in the midst of youth and night,
To look upon me, who before did lie
    Weltring in sinne,

    I felt a sugred strange delight,
Passing all cordials made by any art,
Bedew, embalme, and overrunne my heart,
    And take it in.

Since that time many a bitter storm
My soul hath felt, ev'n able to destroy,
Had the malicious and ill-meaning harm
        His swing and sway;
    But still Thy sweet originall joy,
Sprung from Thine eye, did work within my soul,
And surging griefs, when they grew bold, controll,
        And got the day.

If Thy first glance so powerfull be –
A mirth but open'd, and seal'd up again –
What wonders shall we feel when we shall see
        Thy full-ey'd love!
    When Thou shalt look us out of pain,
And one aspect of Thine spend in delight
More then a thousand sunnes disburse in light,
        In heav'n above.

The Twenty-Third Psalme

The God of love my Shepherd is,
    And He that doth me feed,
While He is mine, and I am His,
    What can I want or need?

He leads me to the tender grasse,
    Where I both feed and rest;
Then to the streams that gently passe:
    In both I have the best.

Or if I stray, He doth convert,
    And bring my minde in frame:
And all this not for my desert,
    But for His holy name.

Yea, in Death's shadie black abode
    Well may I walk, not fear;
For Thou art with me, and Thy rod
    To guide, Thy staffe to bear.

Nay, Thou dost make me sit and dine
   Ev'n in my enemies' sight;
My head with oyl, my cup with wine
   Runnes over day and night.

Surely Thy sweet and wondrous love
   Shall measure all my dayes;
And as it never shall remove,
   So neither shall my praise.

Marie Magdalene

When blessèd Marie wip'd her Saviour's feet –
Whose precepts she had trampled on before –
And wore them for a jewell on her head,
   Shewing His steps should be the street
   Wherein she thenceforth evermore
With pensive humblenesse would live and tread;

She being stain'd herself, why did she strive
To make Him clean Who could not be defil'd?
Why kept she not her tears for her own faults,
   And not His feet? Though we could dive
   In tears like seas, our sinnes are pil'd
Deeper then they, in words, and works, and thoughts.

Deare soul, she knew Who did vouchsafe and deigne
To bear her filth, and that her sinnes did dash
Ev'n God Himself; wherefore she was not loth,
   As she had brought wherewith to stain,
   So to bring in wherewith to wash:
And yet in washing one she washèd both.

Aaron

Holinesse on the head,
  Light and perfections on the breast,
Harmonious bells below, raising the dead
  To leade them unto life and rest:
    Thus are true Aarons drest:

Profanenesse in my head,
  Defects and darknesse in my breast,
A noise of passions ringing me for dead
  Unto a place where is no rest:
    Poore priest, thus am I drest.

Onely another head
  I have, another heart and breast,
Another musick, making live, not dead,
  Without Whom I could have no rest:
    In Him I am well drest.

Christ is my onely head,
  My alone onely heart and breast,
My onely musick, striking me ev'n dead,
  That to the old man I may rest,
    And be in Him new-drest.

So, holy in my head,
  Perfect and light in my deare breast,
My doctrine tun'd by Christ, Who is not dead,
  But lives in me while I do rest,
    Come, people; Aaron's drest.

The Odour

2 Corinthians XI

How sweetly doth 'My Master' sound! 'My Master!'
　　As amber-greese leaves a rich scent
　　　Unto the taster,
　　So do these words a sweet content,
An orientall fragrancie, 'My Master.'

With these all day I do perfume my minde,
　　My minde ev'n thrust into them both;
　　　That I might finde
　　What cordials make this curious broth,
This broth of smells, that feeds and fats my minde.

'My Master,' shall I speak? O that to Thee
　　'My servant' were a little so,
　　　As flesh may be;
　　That these two words might creep and grow
To some degree of spicinesse to Thee!

Then should the pomander, which was before
　　A speaking sweet, mend by reflection,
　　　And tell me more;
　　For pardon of my imperfection
Would warm and work it sweeter then before.

For when 'My Master,' which alone is sweet,
　　And ev'n in my unworthinesse pleasing,
　　　Shall call and meet,
　　'My servant,' as Thee not displeasing,
That call is but the breathing of the sweet.

This breathing would with gains, by sweetning me –
　　As sweet things traffick when they meet –
　　　Return to Thee;
　　And so this new commerce and sweet
Should all my life employ and busie me.

The Foil

If we could see below
The sphere of Vertue and each shining grace
 As plainly as that above doth show,
This were the better skie, the brighter place.

 God hath made starres the foil
To set off vertues, griefs to set off sinning;
 Yet in this wretched world we toil,
As if grief were not foul, nor vertue winning.

The Forerunners

The harbingers are come: see, see their mark;
White is their colour, and behold my head.
But must they have my brain? must they dispark
Those sparkling notions which therein were bred?
 Must dulnesse turn me to a clod?
Yet have they left me, 'Thou art still my God.'

Good men ye be to leave me my best room,
Ev'n all my heart, and what is lodgèd there:
I passe not, I, what of the rest become,
So 'Thou art still my God' be out of fear.
 He will be pleasèd with that dittie;
And if I please Him, I write fine and wittie.

Farewell, sweet phrases, lovely metaphors:
But will ye leave me thus? when ye before
Of stews and brothels onely knew the doores,
Then did I wash you with my tears, and more,
 Brought you to Church well-drest and clad:
My God must have my best, ev'n all I had.

Lovely enchanting language, sugar-cane,
Hony of roses, whither wilt thou flie?
Hath some fond lover tie'd thee to thy bane?
And wilt thou leave the Church, and love a stie?
 Fie! thou wilt soil thy broider'd coat,
And hurt thyself and him that sings the note.

Let foolish lovers, if they will love dung,
With canvas, not with arras, clothe their shame;
Let Follie speak in her own native tongue:
True Beautie dwells on high; ours is a flame
    But borrow'd thence to light us thither:
Beautie and beauteous words should go together.

Yet if you go, I passe not; take your way:
For 'Thou art still my God' is all that ye
Perhaps with more embellishment can say.
Go, birds of Spring; let Winter have his fee;
    Let a bleak palenesse chalk the doore,
So all within be livelier then before.

The Rose

Presse me not to take more pleasure
    In this world of sugred lies,
And to use a larger measure
    Then my strict yet welcome size.

First, there is no pleasure here:
    Colour'd griefs indeed there are,
Blushing woes that look as cleare
    As if they could beautie spare.

Or if such deceits there be —
    Such delights I meant to say —
There are no such things to me,
    Who have pass'd my right away.

But I will not much oppose
    Unto what you now advise;
Onely take this gentle rose,
    And therein my answer lies.

What is fairer then a rose?
    What is sweeter? yet it purgeth.
Purgings enmitie disclose,
    Enmitie forbearance urgeth.

If, then, all that worldlings prize
    Be contracted to a rose,
Sweetly there indeed it lies,
    But it biteth in the close.

So this flower doth judge and sentence
    Worldly joyes to be a scourge;
For they all produce repentance,
    And repentance is a purge.

But I health, not physick, choose:
    Onely, though I you oppose,
Say that fairly I refuse,
    For my answer is a rose.

Discipline

Throw away Thy rod,
Throw away Thy wrath;
           O my God,
Take the gentle path.

For my heart's desire
Unto Thine is bent;
         I aspire
To a full consent.

Nor a word or look
I affect to own,
         But by book,
And Thy Book alone.

Though I fail, I weep;
Though I halt in pace,
         Yet I creep
To the throne of grace.

Then let wrath remove,
Love will do the deed;
         For with love
Stonie hearts will bleed.

Love is swift of foot;
Love's a man of warre,
                              And can shoot,
And can hit from farre.

Who can scape his bow?
That which wrought on Thee,
                              Brought Thee low,
Needs must work on me.

Throw away Thy rod:
Though man frailties hath,
                              Thou art God;
Throw away Thy wrath.

The Invitation

Come ye hither, all whose taste
                              Is your waste;
Save your cost and mend your fare;
God is here prepar'd and drest,
                              And the feast,
God, in Whom all dainties are.

Come ye hither, all whom wine
                              Doth define,
Naming you not to your good;
Weep what ye have drunk amisse,
                              And drink this,
Which, before ye drink, is bloud.

Come ye hither, all whom pain
                              Doth arraigne,
Bringing all your sinnes to sight;
Taste and fear not: God is here
                              In this cheer,
And on sinne doth cast the fright.

Come ye hither, all whom joy
           Doth destroy,
While ye graze without your bounds;
Here is joy that drowneth quite
           Your delight,
As a floud the lower grounds.

Come ye hither, all whose love
           Is your dove,
And exalts you to the skie:
Here is love, which, having breath
           Ev'n in death,
After death can never die.

Lord, I have invited all,
           And I shall
Still invite, still call to Thee;
For it seems but just and right
           In my sight,
Where is all, there all should be.

The Banquet

Welcome, sweet and sacred cheer,
           Welcome deare;
With me, in me, live and dwell:
For thy neatnesse passeth sight,
           Thy delight
Passeth tongue to taste or tell.

O what sweetnesse from the bowl
           Fills my soul,
Such as is and makes divine!
Is some starre – fled from the sphere –
           Melted there,
As we sugar melt in wine?

Or hath sweetnesse in the bread
Made a head
To subdue the smell of sinne;
Flowers, and gummes, and powders giving
All their living,
Lest the enemie should winne?

Doubtlesse neither starre nor flower
Hath the power
Such a sweetnesse to impart;
Onely God, Who gives perfumes,
Flesh assumes,
And with it perfumes my heart.

But as pomanders and wood
Still are good,
Yet being bruis'd are better scented;
God, to show how farre His love
Could improve,
Here, as broken, is presented.

When I had forgot my birth,
And on Earth
In delights of Earth was drown'd,
God took bloud, and needs would be
Spilt with me,
And so found me on the ground.

Having rais'd me to look up,
In a cup
Sweetly He doth meet my taste;
But I still being low and short,
Farre from Court,
Wine becomes a wing at last.

For with it alone I flie
To the skie;
Where I weep mine eyes, and see
What I seek for, what I sue;
Him I view
Who hath done so much for me.

Let the wonder of this pitie
          Be my dittie,
And take up my lines and life;
Hearken under pain of death,
          Hands and breath,
Strive in this, and love the strife.

The Posie

     Let wits contest,
And with their words and posies windows fill;
     'Lesse then the least
Of all Thy mercies' is my posie still.

     This on my ring,
This by my picture, in my book I write;
     Whether I sing,
Or say, or dictate, this is my delight.

     Invention, rest;
Comparisons, go play; wit, use thy will,
     'Lesse then the least
Of all God's mercies' is my posie still.

A Parodie

Soul's joy, when Thou art gone,
        And I alone,
        Which cannot be,
Because Thou dost abide with me,
        And I depend on Thee;

Yet when Thou dost suppresse
        The cheerfulnesse
        Of Thy abode,
And in my powers not stirre abroad,
        But leave me to my load, –

O what a damp and shade
        Doth me invade!
        No stormie night
Can so afflict, or so affright,
      As Thy eclipsèd light.

Ah, Lord, do not withdraw,
        Lest want of aw
        Make sinne appeare,
And when Thou dost but shine lesse cleare,
      Say that Thou art not here.

And then what life I have,
        While Sinne doth rave,
        And falsly boast,
That I may seek, but Thou art lost,
      Thou and alone Thou know'st.

O what a deadly cold
        Doth me infold!
        I half beleeve
That Sinne says true; but while I grieve,
      Thou com'st and dost relieve.

The Elixer

    Teach me, my God and King,
    In all things Thee to see,
And what I do in any thing
    To do it as for Thee.

    Not rudely, as a beast,
    To runne into an action
But still to make Thee prepossest,
    And give it his perfection.

    A man that looks on glasse,
    On it may stay his eye;
Or if he pleaseth, through it passe,
    And then the heav'n espie.

All may of Thee partake:
Nothing can be so mean
Which with his tincture, 'for Thy sake,'
Will not grow bright and clean.

A servant with this clause
Makes drudgerie divine;
Who sweeps a room as for Thy laws
Makes that and th' action fine.

This is the famous stone
That turneth all to gold;
For that which God doth touch and own
Cannot for lesse be told.

A Wreath

A wreathèd garland of deservèd praise,
Of praise deservèd, unto Thee I give,
I give to Thee, Who knowest all my wayes,
My crookèd winding wayes, wherein I live –
Wherein I die, not live; for life is straight,
Straight as a line, and ever tends to Thee –
To Thee, Who art more farre above deceit
Then deceit seems above simplicitie.
Give me simplicitie, that I may live;
So live and like, that I may know Thy wayes
Know them, and practise them; then shall I give,
For this poore wreath, give Thee a crown of praise.

Death

Death, thou wast once an uncouth hideous thing,
          Nothing but bones,
       The sad effect of sadder grones:
Thy mouth was open, but thou couldst not sing.

For we consider'd thee as at some six
          Or ten yeares hence,
       After the losse of life and sense;
Flesh being turned to dust, and bones to sticks.

We lookt on this side of thee, shooting short,
          Where we did finde
       The shells of fledge souls left behinde;
Dry dust, which sheds no tears, but may extort.

But since our Saviour's death did put some bloud
          Into thy face,
       Thou art grown fair and full of grace,
Much in request, much sought for, as a good.

For we do now behold thee gay and glad,
          As at doom's-day,
       When souls shall wear their new aray,
And all thy bones with beautie shall be clad.

Therefore we can go die as sleep, and trust
          Half that we have
       Unto an honest faithfull grave,
Making our pillows either down or dust.

Doom's-Day

Come away,
Make no delay;
Summon all the dust to rise,
Till it stirre and rubbe the eyes,
While this member jogs the other,
Each one whispring, 'Live you, brother?'

Come away,
Make this the day.
Dust, alas, no musick feels
But Thy trumpet; then it kneels,
As peculiar notes and strains
Cure tarantulae's raging pains.

Come away,
O make no stay!
Let the graves make their confession,
Lest at length they plead possession:
Fleshe's stubbornnesse may have
Read that lesson to the grave.

Come away,
Thy flock doth stray.
Some to windes their bodie lend,
And in them may drown a friend;
Some in noisome vapours grow
To a plague and publick wo.

Come away,
Help our decay.
Man is out of order hurl'd,
Parcel'd out to all the world.
Lord, Thy broken consort raise,
And the musick shall be praise.

Judgment

Almightie Judge, how shall poore wretches brook
      Thy dreadfull look,
Able a heart of iron to appall,
      When Thou shalt call
   For ev'ry man's peculiar book?

What others mean to do, I know not well:
      Yet I heare tell
That some will turn Thee to some leaves therein
      So void of sinne,
   That they in merit shall excell.

But I resolve, when Thou shalt call for mine,
      That to decline,
And thrust a Testament into Thy hand:
      Let that be scann'd.
   There Thou shalt find my faults are Thine.

Heaven

O who will show me those delights on high?
      Echo. *I.*
Thou, Echo, thou art mortall, all men know.
      Echo. *No.*
Wert thou not born among the trees and leaves?
      Echo. *Leaves.*
And are there any leaves that still abide?
      Echo. *Bide.*
What leaves are they? impart the matter wholly.
      Echo. *Holy.*
Are holy leaves the Echo, then, of blisse?
      Echo. *Yes.*
Then tell me, what is that supreme delight?
      Echo. *Light.*
Light to the minde: what shall the will enjoy?
      Echo. *Joy.*
But are there cares and businesse with the pleasure?
      Echo. *Leisure.*
Light, joy, and leisure; but shall they persever?
      Echo. *Ever.*

Love

Love bade me welcome; yet my soul drew back,
    Guiltie of dust and sinne.
But quick-ey'd Love, observing me grow slack
    From my first entrance in,
Drew nearer to me, sweetly questioning
    If I lack'd any thing.

'A guest,' I answer'd, 'worthy to be here':
    Love said, 'You shall be he.'
'I, the unkind, ungrateful? Ah, my dear,
    I cannot look on Thee.'
Love took my hand, and smiling did reply,
    'Who made the eyes but I?'

'Truth, Lord; but I have marr'd them; let my shame
    Go where it doth deserve.'
'And know you not,' says Love, 'Who bore the blame?'
    'My dear, then I will serve.'
'You must sit down,' says Love, 'and taste My meat.'
    So I did sit and eat.

FINIS

Glorie be to God on High,
and on earth
Peace, good-will towards men.

THE CHURCH MILITANT

The Church Militant

Almightie Lord, Who from Thy glorious throne
Seest and rulest all things ev'n as one;
The smallest ant or atome knows Thy power,
Known also to each minute of an houre:
Much more do Common-weals acknowledge Thee,
And wrap their policies in Thy decree,
Complying with Thy counsels, doing nought
Which doth not meet with an eternall thought.
But above all, Thy Church and Spouse doth prove,
Not the decrees of power, but bands of love.
Early didst Thou arise to plant this vine,
Which might the more indeare it to be Thine.
Spices come from the East, so did Thy Spouse,
Trimme as the light, sweet as the laden boughs
Of Noah's shadie vine, chaste as the dove,
Prepar'd and fitted to receive Thy love.
The course was westward, that the sunne might light
As well our understanding as our sight.
Where th' Ark did rest, there Abraham began
To bring the other Ark from Canaan.
Moses pursu'd this; but King Solomon
Finish'd and fixt the old religion.
When it grew loose, the Jews did hope in vain
By nailing Christ to fasten it again;
But to the Gentiles He bore Crosse and all,
Rending with earthquakes the partition-wall.
Onely whereas the Ark in glorie shone,
Now with the Crosse, as with a staffe, alone,
Religion, like a pilgrime, Westward bent,
Knocking at all doores ever as She went.
Yet as the sunne, though forward be his flight,
Listens behinde him, and allows some light
Till all depart; so went the Church her way,
Letting, while one foot stept, the other stay
Among the Eastern nations for a time,
Till both removèd to the Western clime.

To Egypt first she came, where they did prove
Wonders of Anger once, but now of Love;
The Ten Commandments there did flourish more
Then the ten bitter plagues had done before;
Holy Macarius and great Anthonie
Made Pharaoh Moses, changing th' historie;
Goshen was darknesse, Egypt full of lights,
Nilus for monsters brought forth Israelites.
Such power hath mightie Baptisme to produce
For things misshapen, things of highest use.
How deare to me, O God, Thy counsels are!
                    Who may with Thee compare?
   Religion thence fled into Greece, where arts
Gave her the highest place in all men's hearts,
Learning was pos'd, Philosophie was set,
Sophisters taken in a fisher's net.
Plato and Aristotle were at a losse,
And wheel'd about again to spell Christ-Crosse.
Prayers chas'd syllogismes into their den,
And Ergo was transform'd into Amen.
Though Greece took horse as soon as Egypt did,
And Rome as both, yet Egypt faster rid,
And spent her period and prefixed time
Before the other. Greece being past her prime,
Religion went to Rome, subduing those
Who, that they might subdue, made all their foes.
The Warrier his deere skarres no more resounds,
But seems to yeeld Christ hath the greater wounds;
Wounds willingly endur'd to work his blisse,
Who by an ambush lost his Paradise.
The great heart stoops, and taketh from the dust,
A sad repentance, not the spoils of lust;
Quitting his spear, lest it should pierce again
Him in His members, Who for him was slain.
The Shepherd's hook grew to a sceptre here,
Giving new names and numbers to the yeare;
But th' Empire dwelt in Greece, to comfort them
Who were cut short in Alexander's stemme.
In both of these Prowesse and Arts did tame
And tune men's hearts against the Gospel came;

Which using, and not fearing skill in th' one,
Or strength in th' other, did erect her throne.
Many a rent and struggling th' Empire knew –
As dying things are wont – untill it flew
At length to Germanie, still Westward bending,
And there the Churche's festivall attending;
That as before Empire and Arts made way –
For no lesse Harbingers would serve then they –
So they might still, and point us out the place
Where first the Church should raise her downcast face.
Strength levels grounds, Art makes a garden there;
Then showres Religion, and makes all to bear.
Spain in the Empire shar'd with Germanie,
But England in the higher victorie,
Giving the Church a crown to keep her state,
And not go lesse then she had done of late.
Constantine's British line meant this of old,
And did this mysterie wrap up and fold
Within a sheet of paper, which was rent
From Time's great Chronicle, and hither sent.
Thus both the Church and sunne together ran
Unto the farthest old meridian.
How deare to me, O God, Thy counsels are!
                         Who may with Thee compare?
   Much about one and the same time and place,
Both where and when the Church began her race,
Sinne did set out of Eastern Babylon,
And travell'd Westward also: journeying on
He chid the Church away where e're he came,
Breaking her peace and tainting her good name.
At first he got to Egypt, and did sow
Gardens of gods, which ev'ry yeare did grow
Fresh and fine deities. They were at great cost,
Who for a god clearely a sallet lost.
Ah, what a thing is man devoid of grace,
Adoring garlick with an humble face,
Begging his food of that which he may eat,
Starving the while he worshippeth his meat!
Who makes a root his god, how low is he,
If God and man be sever'd infinitely!

What wretchednesse can give him any room,
Whose house is foul, while he adores his broom?
None will beleeve this now, though money be
In us the same transplanted foolerie.
Thus Sinne in Egypt sneakèd for a while;
His highest was an ox or crocodile,
And such poore game. Thence he to Greece doth passe.
And being craftier much then Goodnesse was,
He left behinde him garrisons of sinnes,
To make good that which ev'ry day he winnes.
Here Sinne took heart, and for a garden-bed
Rich shrines and oracles he purchased;
He grew a gallant, and would needs foretell
As well what should befall as what befell;
Nay, he became a poet, and would serve
His pills of sublimate in that conserve.
The world came both with hands and purses full
To this great lotterie, and all would pull.
But all was glorious cheating, brave deceit,
Where some poore truths were shuffl'd for a bait
To credit him, and to discredit those
Who after him should braver truths disclose.
From Greece he went to Rome; and as before
He was a god, now he's an emperour;
Nero and others lodg'd him bravely there,
Put him in trust to rule the Romane sphere.
Glorie was his chief instrument of old;
Pleasure succeeded straight when that grew cold,
Which soon was blown to such a mightie flame,
That though our Saviour did destroy the game,
Disparking oracles and all their treasure,
Setting affliction to encounter pleasure;
Yet did a rogue, with hope of carnall joy,
Cheat the most subtill nations. Who so coy,
So trimme, as Greece and Egypt? Yet their hearts
Are given over, for their curious arts,
To such Mahometan stupidities
As the old heathen would deem prodigies.
How deare to me, O God, Thy counsels are!
                    Who may with Thee compare?

Onely the West and Rome do keep them free
From this contagious infidelitie;
And this is all the Rock whereof they boast,
As Rome will one day finde unto her cost;
Sinne being not able to extirpate quite
The Churches here, bravely resolv'd one night
To be a Churchman too, and wear a mitre;
The old debauchèd ruffian would turn writer.
I saw him in his studie, where he sate
Busie in controversies sprung of late:
A gown and pen became him wondrous well;
His grave aspect had more of heav'n then hell;
Onely there was a handsome picture by,
To which he lent a corner of his eye.
As Sinne in Greece a prophet was before,
And in old Rome a mightie emperour;
So now, being priest, he plainly did professe
To make a jest of Christ's three offices;
The rather since his scatter'd jugglings were
United now in one both time and sphere.
From Egypt he took pettie deities,
From Greece oracular infallibilities,
And from old Rome the libertie of pleasure,
By free dispensings of the Churche's treasure;
Then, in memoriall of his ancient throne,
He did surname his palace Babylon.
Yet that he might the better gain all nations,
And make that name good by their transmigrations,
From all these places, but at divers times,
He took fine vizards to conceal his crimes:
From Egypt anchorisme and retirednesse,
Learning from Greece, from old Rome statelinesse;
And blending these, he carri'd all men's eyes,
While Truth sat by, counting his victories;
Whereby he grew apace, and scorn'd to use
Such force as once did captivate the Jews,
But did bewitch, and finally work each nation
Into a voluntarie transmigration.
All poste to Rome; princes submit their necks
Either t' his publick foot or private tricks.

It did not fit his gravitie to stirre,
Nor his long journey, nor his gout and furre;
Therefore he sent out able ministers,
Statesmen within, without doores cloisterers;
Who, without spear, or sword, or other drumme
Then what was in their tongue, did overcome;
And having conquer'd, did so strangely rule,
That the whole world did seem but the Pope's mule.
As new and old Rome did one Empire twist,
So both together are one Antichrist;
Yet with two faces, as their Janus was,
Being in this their old crackt looking-glasse.
How deare to me, O God, Thy counsels are!
                    Who may with Thee compare?
    Thus Sinne triumphs in Western Babylon;
Yet not as Sinne, but as Religion.
Of his two thrones he made the latter best,
And to defray his journey from the East.
Old and new Babylon are to hell and night
As is the moon and sunne to heav'n and light.
When th' one did set, the other did take place,
Confronting equally the Law and Grace.
They are hell's landmarks, Satan's double crest;
They are Sinne's nipples, feeding th' East and West.
But as in vice the copie still exceeds
The pattern, but not so in vertuous deeds;
So, though Sinne made his latter seat the better,
The latter Church is to the first a debter.
The second Temple could not reach the first;
And the late Reformation never durst
Compare with ancient times and purer yeares,
But in the Jews and us deserveth tears.
Nay, it shall ev'ry yeare decrease and fade,
Till such a darknesse do the world invade
At Christ's last coming as His first did finde:
Yet must there such proportions be assign'd
To these diminishings as is between
The spacious world and Jurie to be seen.
Religion stands on tiptoe in our land,
Readie to passe to the American strand.

When height of malice and prodigious lusts,
Impudent sinning, witchcrafts, and distrusts –
The marks of future bane – shall fill our cup
Unto the brimme, and make our measure up;
When Sein shall swallow Tiber, and the Thames,
By letting in them both, pollutes her streams;
When Italie of us shall have her will,
And all her calendar of sinnes fulfill,
Whereby one may foretell what sinnes next yeare
Shall both in France and England domineer –
Then shall Religion to America flee;
They have their times of Gospel ev'n as we.
My God, Thou dost prepare for them a way,
By carrying first their gold from them away;
For gold and grace did never yet agree:
Religion alwaies sides with povertie.
We think we rob them, but we think amisse,
We are more poore, and they more rich by this.
Thou wilt revenge their quarrell, making grace
To pay our debts, and leave our ancient place
To go to them, while that which now their nation
But lends to us, shall be our desolation.
Yet as the Church shall thither Westward flie,
So Sinne shall trace and dog her instantly;
They have their period also and set times,
Both for their vertuous actions and their crimes.
And where of old the Empire and the Arts
Usher'd the Gospel ever in men's hearts,
Spain hath done one; when Arts perform the other,
The Church shall come, and Sinne the Church shall
     smother;
That when they have accomplishèd the round,
And met in th' East their first and ancient sound,
Judgement may meet them both and search them round.
Thus do both lights, as well in Church as Sunne,
Light one another and together runne;
Thus also Sinne and Darknesse follow still
The Church and Sunne with all their power and skill.
But as the Sunne still goes both West and East,
So also did the Church by going West

Still Eastward go; because it drew more neare
To time and place where judgement shall appeare.
How deare to me, O God, Thy counsels are!
                Who may with Thee compare?

L'envoy

King of glorie, King of peace,
With the one make warre to cease;
With the other blesse Thy sheep,
Thee to love, in Thee to sleep.
Let not Sinne devoure Thy fold,
Bragging that Thy bloud is cold;
That Thy death is also dead,
While his conquests dayly spread;
That Thy flesh hath lost his food,
And Thy Crosse is common wood.
Choke him, let him say no more,
But reserve his breath in store,
Till Thy conquests and his fall
Make his sighs to use it all;
And then bargain with the winde
To discharge what is behinde.

Blessed be God alone,
Thrice blessed Three in One.

ADDITIONAL SACRED POEMS

I. *The Holy Communion*

O Gratious Lord, how shall I know
Whether in these gifts Thou bee so
   As Thou art everywhere?
Or rather so, as Thou alone
Tak'st all ye Lodging, leaving none
   For Thy poore creature there.

First I am sure, whether bread stay,
Or whether Bread doe fly away,
   Concerneth Bread, not mee;
But y't both Thou and all Thy traine
Bee there, to Thy truth and my gaine
   Concerneth mee and Thee.

And if in comming to Thy foes,
Thou dost come first to them, y't showes
   The hast of Thy good will;
Or if that Thou two stations makest,
In Bread and mee, the way Thou takest
   Is more, but for mee still.

Then of this also I am sure,
That Thou didst all these pains endure
   To abolish Sinn, not Wheat;
Creatures are good, and have their place;
Sinn onely, w'ch did all deface,
   Thou drivest from his seat.

I could beleeve an Impanation
At the rate of an Incarnation,
   If Thou hadst dyde for Bread;
But that w'ch made my soule to dye,
My flesh and fleshy villany,
   That allso made Thee dead.

That flesh is there mine eyes deny:
And what should flesh but flesh discry –
          The noblest sence of five?
If glorious bodies pass the sight,
Shall they be food and strength and might,
          Euen there where they deceiue?

Into my soule this cannot pass;
Flesh, though exalted, keeps his grass,
          And cannot turn to soule.
Bodyes and Minds are different spheres;
Nor can they change their bounds and meres,
          But keep a constant Pole.

This gift of all gifts is the best,
Thy flesh the least y't I request;
          Thou took'st that pledge from mee:
Give mee not that I had before,
Or give mee that so I have more;
          My God, give mee all Thee.

II. *Love*

Thou art too hard for me in Love;
There is no dealing w'th Thee in that Art,
          That is Thy Masterpeece, I see.
     When I contrive and plott to prove
Something that may be conquest on my part,
          Thou still, O Lord, outstrippest mee.

Sometimes, when as I wash, I say,
And shrodely as I think, 'Lord, wash my soule,
          More spotted then my Flesh can bee.'
     But then there comes into my way
Thy ancient baptism, w'ch when I was foule
          And knew it not, yet cleansèd mee.

I took a time when Thou didst sleep,
Great waves of trouble combating my brest:
  I thought it braue to praise Thee then;
  Yet then I found that Thou didst creep
Into my hart w'th ioye, giving more rest
  Than flesh did lend Thee back agen.

  Let mee but once the conquest have
Vpon ye matter, 'twill Thy conquest prove:
  If Thou subdue mortalitie,
  Thou dost no more than doth ye graue;
Whereas if I orecome Thee and Thy love,
  Hell, Death, and Divel come short of mee.

III. *Trinity Sunday*

He that is one
    Is none;
  Two reacheth Thee
  In some degree:
  Nature and Grace
W'th Glory may attaine Thy Face.
  Steele and a flint strike fire;
  Witt and desire
  Never to Thee aspire,
Except life catch and hold those fast.
  That w'ch beleefe
  Did not confess in ye first Theefe
    His fall can tell
From Heaven through Earth to Hell.
  Lett two of those alone
    To them that fall,
Who God and Saints and Angels loose at last:
  Hee that has one
    Has all.

IV. *Even-Song*

The Day is spent, and hath his will on mee:
    I and ye Sunn haue runn our races:
    I went ye slower, yet more paces;
For I decay, not hee.

Lord, make my Loss vp, and sett mee free,
    That I, who cannot now by day
    Look on his daring brightnes, may
Shine then more bright then hee.

If Thou deferr this light, then shadow mee,
    Least that the Night, earth's gloomy shade,
    Fouling her nest, my earth invade,
As if shades knew not Thee.

But Thou art Light and darkness both togeather:
    If that bee dark we cannot see,
    The sunn is darker then a tree,
And Thou more dark then either.

Yet Thou art not so dark since I know this,
    But that my darknes may touch Thine;
    And hope that may teach it to shine,
Since Light Thy darknes is.

O lett my Soule, whose keyes I must deliver
    Into the hands of senceles dreams
    W'ch know not Thee, suck in Thy beams,
And wake w'th Thee for ever.

V. *The Knell*

The Bell doth tolle:
Lord, help Thy servant, whose perplexed Soule
Doth wishly look
On either hand,
And sometimes offers, sometimes makes a stand,
Struggling on th' hook.
Now is the season,
Now ye great combat of our flesh and reason:
O help, my God;
See, they break in,
Disbanded humours, sorrows, troops of Sinn,
Each w'th his rodd.
Lord, make Thy Blood
Convert and colour all the other flood
And streams of grief,
That they may bee
Julips and cordials when wee call on Thee
For some relief.

VI. *Perseverance*

My God, ye poore expressions of my Love,
W'ch warme these lines and serve them vp to Thee,
Are so as for the present I did moue,
Or rather as Thou mouèdst mee.

But what shall issue, whether these my words
Shall help another, but my iudgment bee;
As a burst fouling-peece doth saue ye birds,
But kill the man, is seal'd w'th Thee.

For who can tell, though Thou hast dyde to winn
And wedd my soule in glorious paradise,
Whither my many crymes and vse of sinn
May yet forbid the banes and bliss?

Onely my soule hangs on Thy promisses,
W'th face and hands clinging vnto Thy brest,
Clinging and crying, crying w'thout cease,
    'Thou art my Rock, Thou art my Rest.'

VII. *The Convert*

If ever tears did flow from eyes,
If ever voice was hoarse with cries,
If ever heart was sore with sighs, –
    Let now my eyes, my voice, my heart
    Strive each to play their part.

My eyes, from whence these tears did spring,
Where treach'rous Syrens us'd to sing,
Shall flow no more, untill they bring
    A deluge on my sensual flame,
    And wash away my shame.

My voice, that oft with foolish lays,
With vows and rants and sensless praise,
Frail Beauty's charms to heav'n did raise,
    Henceforth shall only pierce the skies
    In penitential cryes.

My heart, that gave fond thoughts their food –
Till now averse to all that's good,
The Temple where an idol stood,
    Henceforth in sacred flames shall burn,
    And be that idol's urn.

PSALMS

Psalm I

Blest is the man that never would
    In councels of th' ungodly share,
Nor hath in way of sinners stood,
    Nor sitten in the scorner's chair

But in God's Law sets his delight,
    And makes that Law alone to be
His meditation day and night:
    He shall be like an happy tree,

Which, planted by the waters, shall
    With timely fruit still loden stand;
His leaf shall never fade, and all
    Shall prosper that he takes in hand.

The wicked are not so; but they
    Are like the chaff, which from the face
Of earth is driven by winds away,
    And finds no sure abiding place.

Therefore shall not the wicked be
    Able to stand the Judge's doom;
Nor in the safe society
    Of good men shall the wicked come.

For God Himself vouchsafes to know
    The way that right'ous men have gone;
And those ways which the wicked go
    Shall utterly be overthrown.

Psalm II

Why are the heathen swell'd with rage,
    The people vain exploits devise?
The kings and potentates of earth
    Combin'd in one great faction rise?

And taking councels 'gainst the Lord
    And 'gainst His Christ, presume to say,
'Let us in sunder break their bonds,
    And from us cast their cords away.'

But He that sits in heaven shall laugh,
    The Lord Himself shall them deride;
Then shall He speak to them in wrath,
    And in sore anger vex their pride.

'But I am God, and seated King
    On Sion, His most holy hill;
I will declare the Lord's decree,
    Nor can I hide His sacred will.

He said to Me, Thou art My Son,
    This day have I begotten Thee;
Make Thy request, and I will grant,
    The heathen shall Thy portion be.

Thou shalt possess earth's farthest bounds,
    And there an awful sceptre sway;
Whose pow'r shall dash and break them all,
    Like vessels made of brittle clay.'

Now therefore, O ye kings, be wise;
    Be learnèd, ye that judge the earth;
Serve our great God in fear; rejoice,
    But tremble in your highest mirth.

O kiss the Son, lest He be wroth,
    And straight ye perish from the way:
When once His anger burns, thrice blest
    Are all that make the Son their stay.

Psalm III

How are my foes increasèd, Lord!
    many are they that rise
Against me, saying, for my soul
    no help in God there is.
But Thou, O Lord, art still the shield
    of my deliverance;
Thou art my glory, Lord, and He
    that doth my head advance.

I cry'd unto the Lord, He heard
    me from His holy hill;
I laid me down and slept, I wak't;
    for God sustain'd me still.
Aided by Him, I will not fear
    ten thousand enemies,
Nor all the people round about
    that can against me rise.

Arise, O Lord, and rescue me;
    save me, my God, from thrall;
'Tis Thou upon the cheek-bone smit'st
    mine adversaries all.
And Thou hast brok th' ungodly's teeth:
    salvation unto Thee
Belongs, O Lord; Thy blessing shall
    upon Thy people be.

Psalm IV

Lord, hear me when I call on Thee,
    Lord of my righteousness;
O Thou that hast enlargèd me
    when I was in distress.

Have mercy on me, Lord, and hear
    the prayer that I frame;
How long will ye, vain men, convert
    my glory into shame?

How long will ye seek after lies,
    and vanity approve?
But know the Lord Himself doth chuse
    the righteous man to love.

The Lord will hearken unto me
    when I His grace implore;
O learn to stand in awe of Him,
    and sin not any more.

Within your chamber try your hearts;
    offer to God on high
The sacrifice of righteousness,
    and on His grace rely.

Many there are that say, 'O, who
    will show Us good?' But, Lord,
Thy countenance's cheering light
    do Thou to us afford.

For that, O Lord, with perfect joy
    shall more replenish me
Then worldlings joy'd with all their store
    of corn and wine can be.

Therefore will I lie down in peace
    and take my restful sleep;
For Thy protection, Lord, alone
    shall me in safety keep.

Psalm V

Lord, to my words encline Thine ear,
 My meditation weigh;
My King, my God, vouchsafe to hear
 My cry to Thee, I pray.

Thou in the morn shalt hear my mone;
 For in the morn will I
Direct my prayers to Thy throne,
 And thither lift mine eye.

Thou art a God, Whose puritie
 Cannot in sins delight;
No evil, Lord, shall dwell with Thee,
 Nor fools stand in Thy sight.

Thou hat'st those that unjustly do,
 Thou slay'st the men that lye;
The bloody man, the false one too,
 Shall be abhorr'd by Thee.

But in th' abundance of Thy grace
 Will I to Thee draw near,
And toward Thy most holy place
 Will worship Thee in fear.

Lord, lead me in Thy righteousness,
 Because of all my foes;
And to my dym and sinful eyes
 Thy perfect way disclose.

For wickedness their insides are,
 Their mouths no truth retain,
Their throat an open sepulcher,
 Their flattering tongues do fain.

Destroy them, Lord, and by their own
 Bad councels let them fall
In hight of their transgression;
 O Lord, reject them all;

Because against Thy Majesty
   They vainly have rebell'd.
But let all those that trust in Thee
   With perfect joy be fill'd:

Yes, shout for joy for evermore,
   Protected still by Thee;
Let them that do Thy name adore
   In that still joyfull bee.

For God doth righteous men esteem,
   And them for ever bless;
His favour shall encompass them, –
   A shield in their distress.

Psalm VI

Rebuke me not in wrath, O Lord,
   nor in Thine anger chasten me;
O pity me; for I, O Lord,
   am nothing but infirmitie.

O heal me, for my bones are vex'd,
   my soul is troubled very sore;
But, Lord, how long so much perplex'd
   shall I in vain Thy grace implore?

Return, O God, and rescue me,
   my soul for Thy great mercy save;
For who in death remember Thee?
   or who shall praise Thee in the grave?

With groaning I am wearied,
   all night I make my couch to swim,
And water with salt tears my bed;
   my sight with sorrow waxeth dim.

My beauty wears and doth decay,
   because of all mine enemies;
But now from me depart away,
   all ye that work iniquities.

For God Himself hath heard my cry;
  the Lord vouchsafes to weigh my tears;
Yea, He my prayer from on high
  and humble supplication hears.

And now my foes the Lord will blame
  that e'rst so sorely vexèd me,
And put them all to utter shame,
  and to confusion suddainly.

Glory, honour, power, and praise
  To the most glorious Trinity;
As at the first beginning was,
  is now, and to eternity.

Psalm VII

Save me, my Lord, my God, because
  I put my trust in Thee;
From all that persecute my life,
  O Lord, deliver mee.

Lest like a lion swollen with rage
  he do devour my soul;
And peace-meal rent it, while there's none
  his mallice to controul.

If I have done this thing, O Lord,
  if I so guilty be;
If I have ill rewarded him
  that was at peace with me;

Yea, have not oft deliver'd him
  that was my causeless foe;
Then let mine enemie prevail
  unto mine overthrow.

Let him pursue and take my soul,
  yea, let him to the clay
Tread down my life, and in the dust
  my slaughter'd honour lay.

Arise in wrath, O Lord, advance
   against my foes' disdain;
Wake and confirm that judgment now
   which Thou did'st foreordain.

So shall the people round about
   resort to give Thee praise;
For their sakes, Lord, return on high,
   and high Thy glory raise.

The Lord shall judge the people all:
   O God, consider me
According to my righteousness
   and mine integritie.

The wicked's malice, Lord, confound,
   but just me ever guide;
Thou art that righteous God by whom
   the hearts and rains are try'd.

God is my shield, Who doth preserve
   those that in heart are right;
He judgeth both the good and those
   that do His justice slight.

Unless the wicked turn again,
   the Lord will whet His sword;
His bow is bent, His quiver is
   with shafts of vengeance stor'd.

The fatal instruments of death
   in that preparèd lie;
His arrows are ordain'd 'gainst him
   that persecuteth me.

Behold, the wicked travelleth
   with his iniquitie;
Exploits of mischief he conceives,
   but shall bring forth a lye.

The wicked diggèd, and a pit
   for others' ruine wrought;
But in the pit which he hath made
   Shall he himself be caught.

To his own head his wickedness
   shall be returnèd home;
And on his own accursèd pate
   his cruelty shall come.

But I, for all His righteousness,
   the Lord will magnifie;
And ever praise the glorious Name
   of Him that is on high.

Gloria to Psalm XXIII

To Father, Son, and Holy Ghost,
   one consubstantial Three,
All highest praise, all humblest thanks,
   now and for ever be.

SECULAR POEMS

Sonnets

Sent to His Mother as a New Year's Gift From Cambridge

My God, where is that ancient heat towards Thee
    Wherewith whole showls of martyrs once did burn,
Besides their other flames? Doth Poetry
    Wear Venus' livery? only serve her turn?
Why are not sonnets made of Thee, and layes
    Upon Thine altar burnt? Cannot Thy love
Heighten a spirit to sound out Thy praise
    As well as any she? Cannot Thy Dove
Outstrip their Cupid easily in flight?
    Or, since Thy wayes are deep, and still the same,
    Will not a verse run smooth that bears Thy Name?
Why doth that fire, which by Thy power and might
    Each breast does feel, no braver fuel choose
    Then that which one day worms may chance refuse?

Sure, Lord, there is enough in Thee to dry
    Oceans of ink; for, as the Deluge did
Cover the earth, so doth Thy Majesty.
    Each cloud distills Thy praise, and doth forbid
Poets to turn it to another use;
    Roses and lillies speak Thee, and to make
A pair of cheeks of them, is Thy abuse.
    Why should I women's eyes for chrystal take?
Such poor invention burns in their low mind,
    Whose fire is wild, and doth not upward go
   To praise, and on Thee, Lord, some ink bestow.
Open the bones, and you shall nothing find
    In the best face but filth; when, Lord, in Thee
    The beauty lies in the discovery.

Inscription in the Parsonage, Bemerton

To My Successor

If thou chance for to find
A new House to thy mind,
   And built without thy cost;
Be good to the Poor
As God gives thee store,
   And then my Labour's not lost.

Another Version

If thou dost find
An house built to thy mind,
   Without thy cost;
Serve thou the more
God and the poor;
   My labour is not lost.

On Lord Danvers

Sacred marble, safely keepe
His dust who under thee must sleepe
Untill the graves againe restore
Theire dead, and time shal be no more.

Meane while, if Hee which all thinges weares
Doe ruine thee, or if the tears
Are shed for him dissolve thy frame,
Thou art requited; for his fame,
His vertues, and his worth shal bee
Another monument for thee.

On Sir John Danvers

Passe not by;
Search, and you may
Find a treasure
Worth your stay.
What makes a Danvers
Would you find?
In a fayre bodie
A fayre mind.

Sr John Danvers' earthly part
Here is copied out by art;
But his heavenly and divine
In his progenie doth shine.
Had he only brought them forth,
Know that much had been his worth.
Ther's no monument to a sonne;
Read him there, and I have done.

A Paradox

That the Sick are in a Better Case Then the Whole

You who admire yourselves because
    You neither grone nor weepe,
And think it contrary to nature's laws
    To want one ounce of sleepe;
        Your strong beleife
Acquits yourselves, and gives ye sick all greife.

Your state to ours is contrary;
    That makes you thinke us poore:
So Black-Moores think us foule, and wee
    Are quit w'th y'm and more:
        Nothing can see
And judge of things but mediocrity.

The sick are in y'mselves a state
    W'ch health hath nought to doe,
How know you that o'r tears pr'ceed from woe,
    And not fro better fate
        Since that Mirth hath
Her waters alsoe and desyrèd bath.

How know you y't ye sighs wee send
    Fro want of breath pr'ceede,
Not fro excesse? and therefore we do spend
    That w'ch we do not neede:

So trembling may
As well shew inward warbling, as decay.

Cease y'n to judge calamityes
    By outward forme and shew,
But view yourselves, and inward turn yo'r eyes,
    Then you shall fully know
        That your estate
Is, of ye two, ye farre more desperate.

You allwayes feare to feele those smarts
    W'ch we but sometimes pr've;
Each little comfort much affects o'r hearts,
    None but gross joyes you move;
        Why, then confesse
Your feares in number more, yo'r joyes are lesse.

Then for yo'rselves not us embrace
    Plaints to bad fortune due;
For though you visitt us, and plaint o'r case,
    Wee doubt much whether you
        Come to our bed
To comfort us, or to be comforted.

To Ye Queene of Bohemia

Bright soule, of whome if any countrey knowne
Worthy had bin, thou hadst not lost thine owne;
No Earth can bee thy Jointure, For the sunne
And starres alone vnto ye pitch doe runne
And pace of thy swift vertues; onely they
Are thy dominion. Those that rule in clay
Stick fast therein, but thy transcendent soule
Doth for two clods of earth ten spheres controule,
And though starres shott from heauen loose their light,
Yet thy braue beames, excluded from their right,
Maintaine their Lustre still, & shining cleere
Turne watrish Holland to a chrystalline sphere.
Mee thinkes, in that Dutch optick I doe see

Thy curious vertues much more visibly:
There is thy best Throne, for afflictions are
A foile to sett off worth & make it rare.
Through y't black tiffany thy vertues shine
Fairer and richer. Now wee know what's thine,
And what is fortune's. Thou hast singled out
Sorrowes & griefs, to fight with them about
At there owne weapons, w'thout pomp or state
To second thee against their cunning hate.
O what a poore thing 'tis to bee a Queene
When scepters, state, Attendants are ye screene
Betwixt us & the people! when-as glory
Lyes round about us to helpe out ye story,
When all things pull & hale, y't they may bring
A slow behauiour to the style of king;
When sense is made by Comments, But y't face
Whose natiue beauty needs not dresse or lace
To serue it forth, & being stript of all
Is self-sufficient to bee the thrall
Of thousand harts: y't face doth figure thee
And show thy vndiuided Maiestye
W'ch misery cannot vntwist, but rather
Addes to the vnion, as lights doe gather
Splendour from darknes. So close sits ye crowne
About thy temples y't ye furious frowne
Of opposition cannot place thee where
Thou shalt not be a Queene, & conquer there.
Yet hast thou more dominions: God doth giue
Children for kingdomes to thee; they shall liue
To conquer new ones, & shall share ye frame
Of th' vniuerse, like as ye windes, & name
The world anew: ye sunne shall neuer rise
But it shall spy some of their victories.
Their hands shall clipp ye Eagles winges, & chase
Those rauening Harpyes w'ch peck at thy face
At once to Hell, without a baiting while
At Purgatory, their inchanted Ile
And Paris garden. Then let their perfume
And Spanish sents, wisely layd vp, presume
To deale w'th brimstone, y't vntaméd stench

Whose fier, like their malice, nought can quench.
But ioyes are stord for thee; thou shalt returne
Laden w'th comforts thence, where now to morne
Is thy chief gouerment, to manage woe,
To curbe some Rebell teares w'ch faine would flow,
Making a Head & spring against thy Reason.
This is thy empire yet: till better season
Call thee from out of y't surrounded Land;
That habitable sea, & brinish strand,
Thy teares not needing. For y't hand Divine,
W'ch migles water w'th thy Rhenish wine,
Will power full ioyes to thee; but dregs to those
And meet theire tast who are thy bitter foes.

L'envoy

Shine on, Maiestick soule, abide
Like Dauid's tree, planted beside
The Flemmish riuers: in the end
Thy fruite shall w'th their drops contend;
Great God will surely dry those teares,
Which now y't moist land to thee beares.
Then shall thy Glory, fresh as flowers
In water kept, maugre the powers
Of Diuell, Jesuitt, & Spaine,
From Holland saile into the Maine:
Thence wheeling on, it compass shall
This oure great Sublunary Ball,
And with that Ring thy fame shall wedd
Eternity into one Bedd.

INDEX OF POEMS

INDEX OF FIRST LINES